OPERATION TRANSFORMATION

Leader's Guide

A **Vacation Bible School** Curriculum for the Church of the Nazarene, Inc.

Acknowledgments

Rev. Mike Hancock

Tracy Fischer

Zac Fischer

Rev. Bill Hart

Rev. Leslie Hart

DaVonne Lee and family members: Bradly, Bowen, Brynn, Brayah, and Braven

Airborne Audio Productions (Isaac Moreno)
airborneaudio.com

Hide & Keep Ministries (DaVonne Lee)
hideandkeep.com

Skyward Studios (Zac and Tracy Fischer)

Vocals: Christopher Allen, Zac Fischer, DaVonne Lee, Marah Fischer, and Tracy Fischer

Printed by Discipleship Ministries, Mesoamerica Region

www.SdmiResources.MesoamericaRegion.org

ISBN: 978-1-63580-171-2

Table of Contents

Week at a Glance 4

Welcome to *Operation Transformation* 6

Operation Transformation Toolkit 8
- Mission 8
- Theme Memory Verse 8
- What is VBS? 8
- Why Invest in a VBS? 8
- How Can VBS Work? 8
- Strategy 8
- Including Preschoolers 9
- Getting Everyone's Attention Quickly: Top Secret Hand Signal 9
- Prizes and Giveaway Ideas 10
- Sample Daily Schedule 10

Intentional Connections: Before, During, and After VBS 11
- Intentional Connection Activity Plan 11
  1. Connection Activities Prior to VBS 11
  2. Host Connection Activities During VBS 12
  3. Host Connection Activities After VBS Prior to the VBS Celebration Service 12
  4. VBS Celebration Service 12
  5. Connection Activity Ideas After the VBS Celebration Service 13

Prayer 14

Preparing Your Team with Training 15
- *Operation Transformation* Daily Schedule 15
  - Leadership Meeting 15
  - Kids' Arrival 15
  - Opening and Welcome 15
  - Music 15
  - Opening Skit 16
  - Transformation Station Options 16
    - Mission Brief 17
    - Evidence Vault 17
    - Craft Lab 17
    - Recharge Station 17
    - Agent Training Field 17
    - Infiltration Service Project 17
  - Closing Skit 17

Leading a Child to Christ 18
Day One 20
Day Two 50
Day Three 76
Day Four 102
Memory Verse Activities 129
Coloring Pages 140
Graphics, Misc. 147

Week at a Glance

"Do not conform to the pattern of this world, but be transformed by the renewing of your mind..."
Romans 12:2a

	DAY 1	DAY 2	DAY 3	DAY 4
PASSCODE	Jesus' love transforms my identity	Jesus' power transforms my life	Jesus' presence transforms my choices	Jesus' call transforms my mission
FOCUS	Salvation	Sanctification (Initial)	Sustaining	Sending
ICON	Thumbprint	Footprint	Flashlight	Cross
AT A GLANCE FOR TEACHERS	God gives us new life through Jesus. Saul the murderer becomes "Brother Paul" the Christian.	Jesus leads me where I never imagined. As I trust and follow Him, Jesus transforms me.	Jesus is always with me. He equips me with wisdom, provides for my needs, and shows me the next step when I persevere.	God calls me to share my transformation with others.
BIBLE STORY	Saul's transformation Acts 9:1-19	Saul meets the disciples in Jerusalem Acts 9:20-30	God works through Paul in prison Acts 16:16-34	Paul remembers God's call Acts 22:1-16
MEMORY VERSE	Yet to all who did receive him, to those who believed in his name, he gave the right to become children of God. John 1:12	My sheep listen to my voice; I know them, and they follow me. John 10:27	He guides the humble in what is right and teaches them his way. Psalm 25:9	Now this is eternal life: that they know you, the only true God, and Jesus Christ... John 17:3a

	DAY 1	DAY 2	DAY 3	DAY 4
MUSIC	Theme song Today's memory verse song Optional worship song theme: *Jesus our Savior and God's love*	Theme song Today's memory verse song Optional worship song theme: *Jesus our Lord; surrender; or trust*	Theme song Today's memory verse song Optional worship song theme: *Jesus our friend, guide, and strength*	Theme song Today's memory verse song Optional worship song theme: *Jesus our King; our obedience; God's call*
MISSION BRIEF	Flower Power	Caterpillar Soup	Decode God's Perspective	A Tale of Two Balloons!
CRAFT LAB	Identity Badges	Butterfly Footprints	Invisible Ink	Salvation Bracelet
RECHARGE STATION	Road to Damascus	Sheep Snacks	Paul In Prison Snack Mix	Popcorn Transformation
AGENT TRAINING FIELD	Hold On, Saul! (Statues Game)	Follow Me	I Know My Shoe!	Helper and Friend (3-legged Race)
INFILTRATION SERVICE PROJECT	Giving something that points to new life through Jesus	Doing something that will transform someone's day	Being a help and a friend to someone because Jesus is our Help and Friend	Doing something that will share Jesus with others

Welcome to OPERATION TRANSFORMATION!

Dear Vacation Bible School Leader,

Get ready! *Operation Transformation* takes us on an adventure of a lifetime as we learn lessons from Paul's personal journey of transformation through Jesus' love, power, presence, and call!

Paul was earnest in his zeal for God. He was just going in the wrong direction and didn't know it! Paul started on a journey to capture and persecute Christians but found himself captured by Christ Himself. The blinding light, Jesus' voice, and the revelation of God's love transformed Paul's life and his mission!

Operation Transformation invites children to become God's agents-in-training, to be transformed, and to join in the mission to transform the world with the Good News of Jesus. Each day, Special Agent Tre (code name "Trinity") and his sidekick Buddy (code name "Barnabas") will teach kids why it is important to follow Romans 12:2a and "not conform to the pattern of this world but be transformed by the renewing of your mind." Kids will learn that personal transformation affects many other lives and advances God's mission to spread the Good News to the world.

One week at *Operation Transformation* offers kids a TRANSFORMED LIFE!

When children join *Operation Transformation*, they learn a daily passcode that highlights each day's lesson focus. They see an icon throughout the day that will prompt them to say the passcode. The daily song underscores the memory verse, making it easier to memorize. The Transformation Station activities reinforce the lesson themes:

- **Salvation:** Jesus' love transforms my identity and gives me new life as a child of God. (John 1:12)
- **Sanctification (initial):** Jesus' power transforms my life as I trust and follow Him. (John 10:27)
- **Sustaining:** Jesus' presence transforms my choices as He equips me with wisdom, provides for my needs, and shows me the next step when I persevere. (Psalm 25:9)
- **Sending:** Jesus' call transforms my mission as God calls me to share my transformation with others. (John 17:3)

This week, look for opportunities to help children relate to Jesus in these ways:

- As our **Savior** (We accept His free gift and thank Him for coming to rescue us.)
- As our **King** (We follow and obey this King that loves us so much.)
- As our **Friend** (We talk to and listen to our Friend. We love others because we have such a Friend that loves us.)

This curriculum provides scripts, skits, crafts, games, songs, Bible stories, helpful tips, and ideas to communicate and emphasize the message of the Gospel with kids and their families. The activities are optional. Choose what fits best in your setting. This Leader's Guide is a planning and training tool. Use it to help you host a dynamic, fun, and successful Vacation Bible School for your community.

We encourage you to end the week with a Celebration and Connection Service. Share the vision with your pastor and church staff; be sure to enlist their support well in advance. Invite all the *Operation Transformation* kids and their families to join your Sunday morning worship service following VBS. Feature portions of the skit, have the children sing their songs and recite memory verses, and share testimonies of changed lives from leaders, children, and even parents. The goal is to celebrate the Good News of transformation in Jesus Christ! Ask your pastor to close with an invitation to accept God's offer of new life through Jesus.

We are excited about your involvement in Vacation Bible School this year. We believe this ministry is one of the most powerful tools available to reach children and their families for Christ! We know that God will bless your efforts. Know that we have prayed for you and for the children, that they will receive the transforming message of the Gospel throughout this important week.

Your Sunday School & Discipleship Ministries Team,
Church of the Nazarene

OPERATION TRANSFORMATION Toolkit

Mission
To make disciple-makers in all the nations.

Theme Memory Verse
"Do not conform to the pattern of this world but be transformed by the renewing of your mind." Romans 12:2a.

What is VBS?
Typically, VBS is a four- to five-day program that is two to three hours each day. Some churches may choose to have one or two day events. VBS is designed to invite children and their families into a relationship with Jesus. VBS is a tool for the local church to draw others into their church fellowship for the purpose of making disciples in all nations and helping them grow into disciple-makers.

Why invest in a VBS?
Our mission is to reach all children with the Good News of Jesus Christ that they may be transformed by His saving grace, live Christlike lives through the power of Jesus' presence, and share His love to transform the world.

How can VBS work?
Vacation Bible School can be approached in many different ways.
- **Backyard Bible Clubs:** Held at the homes of church members, culminating in a weekend church service or event.
- **On-Site VBS:** Held in the church building, culminating in a weekend church service.
- **Community-Site VBS:** Held in a central location in a target ministry area. This can be in a community center, a playground or park, or a building you rent for the week close to the neighborhood your church is strategically targeting. The activity can culminate in a weekend church service.

Strategy
- To **reach** children and their families in your community with the Good News of Jesus Christ
- To **connect** with children and their families in meaningful, practical, and helpful ways
- To help children **grow** spiritually through Biblical principles
- To provide opportunities to model Christlike **service**

Target Age

The recommended ages are 5 to 12 years old, or Kindergarten to sixth grade.

Including Preschoolers (optional)

Some groups may include a number of preschoolers among them. This can be a very good thing! Since our material is targeted at children Kindergarten through sixth grade, we are asking that preschoolers who attend (and they are welcome to attend!) be accompanied at all times by a parent or guardian. This will give them the security of having a familiar adult near them should they become bored, restless, or fearful.

A few helpful suggestions for including preschoolers in your VBS:

- For liability reasons, parents/guardians of preschoolers MUST accompany them at all times.
- Be sure preschoolers complete a registration form.
- Preschoolers can be included in the Transformation Stations with their parents/guardians to ensure they stay focused and on task.
- If more than three preschoolers attend, consider forming a preschool group that rotates separately to the Transformation Stations.
- Invite the preschoolers and parents who participate in the *Operation Transformation* Celebration to learn more about your preschool ministry.

Getting Everyone's Attention Quickly: The Top Secret Hand Signal (optional)

Teach this top secret hand signal to the children on the first day. It is our sign for everyone to be super quiet because something important is about to happen. Make sure all staff members know it so they can do it with you when you teach the kids.

When they hear a teacher start the signal, they are to stop what they are doing and join in. You can use this anywhere during VBS. It is effective when leaders lead by example and emphasize participation.

Tap-tap, clap-clap, snap-snap, "Shhhhhh!"

Tap-tap: Pat the top of your legs with both palms.

Clap-clap: Clap your hands twice.

Snap-snap: Snap your fingers twice.

"Shhhhhh!": Say, "Shhhhhh" while bringing your index finger in a slow sweeping motion to your lips.

Prizes and Giveaway Ideas (optional)

In order to help kids stay engaged, consider these optional incentives:

1. Print mission money (found in resources) that children can earn each day and spend at the Special Agent Store.
   - Each day, children can earn mission money by:
     - Bringing their Bible (1)
     - Learning their memory verse (1)
     - Participation or answering a question in review or lesson (1)
     - Bringing a friend (2 for each friend)
     - Additional ideas: Act of kindness, listening carefully, keeping hands to yourself, etc. This can be used as an effective tool to reward good behavior.
   - Write the child's name on the back as they earn it.
   - Let them spend their mission money at the Special Agent Store at the end of the day or week.
   - Special Agent Store—Invite your church to donate small toys, school supplies, or candy that the kids can purchase with their mission money.

2. Make a Mission Accomplished Punch Card for each child. Use the same list as the one above for earning mission money. When they reach 10 punches, they can turn the card in for a prize from the Special Agent Store.

3. Have a prize box of donated items (small toys, school supplies, snacks, or candies) children can choose from at the end of each day.

Sample Daily Schedule

3-Hour Onsite Morning Schedule

8:45-9:00	Leaders meeting & prayer
9:00-9:10	Kids arrive
9:05-9:40	Welcome and opening music & skit
9:45-10:15	Transformation Station
10:15-10:45	Transformation Station
10:45-11:15	Transformation Station
11:15-11:45	Transformation Station
11:45-12:00	Closing skit

2-Hour Backyard Club Evening Schedule

6:00-6:15	Leaders meeting & prayer
6:15-6:30	Kids arrive
6:30-6:35	Welcome and opening music & skit
7:00-7:20	Transformation Station
7:20-7:40	Transformation Station
7:40-8:00	Transformation Station
8:00-8:20	Transformation Station
8:20-8:30	Closing skit

These are *suggested* sample schedule options! Choose a schedule that works best for you. This suggested schedule allows the children to hear the story and daily themes before they go to Transformation Stations and provides a biblical review before they leave.

Intentional Connections: Before, During, and After VBS

Create a culture of connections. Our ultimate goal is to help children develop a lifelong relationship with Jesus. We believe that is best accomplished by connecting to a community of believers. Because of this, VBS is a strategic time to identify "prospect families" who may be interested in coming to your church. Prospect families are families not actively attending another church. It is important to recruit host volunteers who will focus on making connections with these families.

On the first day of VBS attendance, your team will identify children of prospect families and connect a VBS host volunteer with that family. The host volunteer will be their host for the week. The host should use each day to develop a relationship with prospect children and parents through conversation and interaction in order to create a connection.

Intentional Connection Activity Plan

Connecting with prospect families begins before VBS and continues after the four days of VBS are over. Consistent connections don't happen accidentally. We must be intentional to create connections:

1. **Prior to VBS:** Host a launch event as an all-church activity.
2. **Monday–Thursday:** VBS. Announce this as an all-church event. Encourage church-wide involvement.
3. **Friday, Saturday, or Sunday:** Use Connection Activities. *(See page 12)*
4. **Sunday:** Hold a VBS Celebration Service. Invite everyone to see what God has done during the week.
5. **After VBS Week:** Use Connection Activities. *(See page 13)*

1. Connection Activities Prior to VBS

- Hand out invitations personally to the parents of children whose lives already intersect with yours. Invite them to VBS by:
  - Going door-to-door in your neighborhood
  - Visiting your children's school
  - Talking to fellow parents of your child's sports team or class
- Send follow-up phone calls or texts. Inform parents if your church is equipped to offer transportation.
- Sponsor a launch event the weekend before VBS to invite families in the church's neighborhood (grill hot dogs or potluck).

2. Host Connection Activities During VBS

- The host volunteer connects with parents after their first day and lets them know how glad they were to have their child/children at VBS and that they are looking forward to having them back.
- If a child/family misses any days during the week, the host volunteer will follow-up to let them know they were missed.
- The host volunteer connects with them in person or by phone, invites them to the celebration service, and plans to attend with them.
- The host volunteer should make efforts to greet the parents of the children at arrival and dismissal times.
- Churches can hold a class or fellowship for parents during VBS.
  - Introduce them to your church, what the Church of the Nazarene believes, what a walk with God looks like, etc.
  - Review what the kids are learning each day.
  - Allow time for parents to ask questions.
  - Provide light snacks (muffins and coffee).
  - Provide childcare for younger siblings to allow parents to participate.
- Encourage kids to put prayer requests in a designated box and pray for each request.

3. Host Connection Activities After VBS Prior to the VBS Celebration Service

- Invite prospect families to Sunday's celebration service and let them know you will be looking for them.
- Tell them the good things you saw in their child ("Tommy has been such a great listener this week" or "I really enjoyed getting to know Sally. Thank you for bringing her this week!")
- Invite them to sit with you at the dinner after the celebration service.

4. VBS Celebration Service

Invite the children and families to attend the Sunday morning worship service at the end of your VBS week. This service should be designed around VBS participation. Intend to reach new seekers. Invite VBS participants to the platform to sing the VBS songs and recite the memory verses. Feature a multi-media recap of the week through videos or a slide show.

IMPORTANT NOTE FOR DIRECTOR: *Before VBS begins,* recruit an artistic director who will assemble a team to document the VBS experience from beginning to end through video, photos, or both, and prepare an edited 3-4 minute VBS video or PowerPoint presentation that will be featured in the VBS Celebration Service.

Plan for a community meal following the service and invite all prospect families and children. Be intentional about seating hosts and leaders among prospect families and children.

5. Connection Activity Ideas After the VBS Celebration Service

- Stop by a prospect family's home briefly with a gift and invite them to join you for church. Here are a few gift ideas:
  - A mug with the church's name filled with candy.
  - A card with your hand-written comments thanking them for bringing their child to VBS and inviting them to church as your personal guest. If you do this, look for them in church. Remember their names. Greet them, introduce them to others, and sit with them in the service. If possible, invite them to be your guest for a meal afterwards.
- Send a text or email checking on their child. "I was just thinking about Tommy and wanted you to know what a joy it was to have him in VBS. He has been on my mind today. Let me know if there is anything I can pray about for him/her or your family."
- If you know the child plays an organized sport, attend one of their games/matches and cheer them on. Connect with the child and parents afterwards.
- Intentionally connect throughout the year, following up every month or so without becoming a nuisance. Invite them to special services (Christmas and Easter) or any age-appropriate activity that your children's ministry is having.
- If you see them in public, address them by name and let them know you care.
- Follow Ephesians 5:16 and "make the most of every opportunity" with these precious children and families.

Prayer

It is never too early to engage your prayer team in VBS!

Anyone can design a fun, entertaining, and engaging VBS. We can stir up excitement about Bible stories and even get people to start coming to our church. But if we want to accomplish more than just entertainment, if we want people to come to know Jesus Himself through our VBS, we will need the Lord to do what only He can do!

Psalm 127:1 says, "Unless the Lord builds the house, the builders labor in vain. Unless the Lord watches over the city, the guards stand watch in vain."

Probably the most important preparation you make for VBS is prayer. Pray:

- For provision (the materials, the prizes, the children that need to hear this message, the families that need this church).

- For inspiration, ideas, creativity, and excitement.

- For the Holy Spirit to be present at every planning meeting and every single moment of VBS.

- For discernment for the leaders and protection of each child.

- For the families that will come to the church through this VBS. If possible, pray for them by name.

- For the church family to be ready for the harvest God is preparing through VBS. That the church would love these people well, and that we would look more and more like Jesus.

- For the story of Paul's life to powerfully communicate God's love and redemption.

- For the Bible to be elevated to its proper place in the children's hearts and minds—that they will see it as a source of strength, wisdom, and comfort.

- For the workers to be granted wisdom to answer the children's questions.

- For the Name of Jesus to be magnified.

- For many to be led to repentance and a deeper relationship with God and others.

- For God's kingdom to come and His will to be done in VBS and beyond.

Preparing your Team with Training

Provide team training at least one month prior to VBS.

- Train Volunteers on Nazarene Safe policies and practices.
- Introduce Transformation Station leaders, skit characters, and other key leaders.
- Teach the secret hand signal.
- Teach all songs and motions.
- Review all elements in the daily schedule.
- Discuss how to lead a child to Christ.

Operation Transformation Daily Schedule

Leadership Meeting

Plan to meet together each day to read the Bible story, review the day, and pray. This meeting is scheduled to last 15 minutes. This is your time to focus as a team. Plan to have all decorating, instruction, preparation, memorizing, reviewing, etc. completed before this opening meeting.

Kids' Arrival

Everyone should greet the children as they arrive. Provide assigned greeters in the parking lot and at the front doors. Show children and parents where to register or check in. Let them know we've been expecting them and are glad they are here.

Opening and Welcome

The director will welcome everyone, review the daily passcode and verse, and make announcements.

Music

A worship leader or team will lead music during the opening and closing sessions, using hand motions to emphasize the words. All of our songs are Bible verses.

ALL adults should fully participate in the singing and hand motions (even if they're tone deaf!). When kids witness non-participating adults, they get the message that participation is optional. All adults present should lead by example through enthusiastic, cheerful participation.

To help the children become familiar with the songs, play the music in the background during transitions from one activity to the next.

The children will be singing this week's VBS songs at the *Operation Transformation* Celebration Service.

We are providing five theme songs and two bonus songs:
1. *Operation Transformation* theme song (Romans 12:2)
2. Day 1 (John 1:12)
3. Day 2 (John 10:27)
4. Day 3 (Psalm 25:9)
5. Day 4 (John 17:3a)
6. Bonus Song 1 (Timothy 6:18)
7. Bonus Song 2 (Psalm 46:1)

You can download them here:
http://www.mesoamericaregion.org/en/package/vacation-bible-school-operation-transformation/

Opening Skit

Dialogue has been provided between three characters to introduce the Bible story. The story is explored in greater depth in the Mission Brief Station. The skit emphasizes the main points of each day's Bible story and demonstrates the joys, responsibilities, and privileges of Christian life through special agent parables.

Skit Characters:

- **Special Agent Tre (Code Name Trinity):** Wears "spy" clothes, hat, and sunglasses.
  - This is your main speaker. A pastor or leader with an engaging personality is the best choice for this part. He or she will be training Buddy (and the kids) about becoming a Christian and growing in Christ.
  - Either a man or a woman can play this part. We will use the pronoun "he" for simplicity's sake in the curriculum. Please feel free to change that if your actor is a female.
  - Regardless of gender, this person needs to be a mature believer; someone the children and parents can respect as a Christian role model even after VBS is over.
- **Agent-in-training Buddy (Code Name Barnabas):** Buddy is a seeker, a clumsy but loveable and curious sidekick who really wants to be a special agent.
- **Agent Strange (Code Name Scout):** The antagonist, an impostor who tries to thwart Tre's missions. Also wears "spy" clothes, hat, and sunglasses. By the end of the week he becomes "Scout" as he responds to God through Special Agent Tre and Buddy.
- **VBS director:** Also a special agent, this person is the VBS master of ceremonies (emcee). Opens and closes, gives direction as needed, and makes sure the schedule is followed.

Transformation Station Options

For large groups, split children into smaller groups by age. Each group has an adult leader to guide them to the appropriate stations according to the schedule. For Backyard Bible Clubs or very small groups, all children can rotate stations together as one large group.

The same person or people should lead the same Transformation Station each day. This provides important continuity and connection. Familiarity gives children a greater sense of security and increases their comfort level. As a bonus, the leader's familiarity with each lesson will help them "connect the dots" between each day's story. Because of the importance of the Mission Brief Station, be sure the same person leads it every day, even if that is not possible for other stations.

Mission Brief

This is the most important Transformation Station. If you only have time for one station, make this the one. This is where children will receive a detailed explanation of the Bible story prefaced in the skit and an object lesson that illuminates the daily theme and verse. The importance of this station cannot be overstated.

Evidence Vault

Teach hand motions to the daily memory verse, explain the meaning of the verse, and answer children's questions about how it applies to them.

Craft Lab

Help the children create something that will reinforce the daily theme.

Recharge Station

Facilitate discussion of the day's Bible story as children enjoy creating and eating a snack that reflects the story or theme.

Agent Training Field

Through physical activity, each game emphasizes the theme or memory verse and points out real-world applications.

Infiltration Service Project

The congregation participates in this option by providing supplies for VBS service projects. These projects have a dual purpose: community outreach and teaching the children the power and importance of loving others through service. Choose service projects that require some physical activity. Multiply the impact of their service time by incorporating and reinforcing the theme for the day. The service project ideas should be adapted to fit your church and community needs. The examples we provide are simply suggestions. (*See page 5 for each day's theme*)

Closing Skit

The director ends the closing skit with announcements, offering totals, and a closing prayer. If time allows, end with singing the daily song.

Leading a Child to Christ

God will bless your availability and your willingness to pray with a child. Let go and let God do the leading. If you are praying at an altar, always ask the child if you can pray with them and if they know what they want to pray about. Sometimes a child may be thinking of a sick pet or family member. Children seeking salvation usually express this by saying, "I want Jesus to be my friend" or "I want to be a Christian."

Once you know a child is seeking a relationship with God, lead the child through the following conversation. You can use this as a script or say it in your own words. Pause periodically and ask if they understand what you are sharing. Start by asking the child the following questions:

1. Do you believe that God loves you?

    God loves you and all people. He wants to have a loving friendship with you. John 3:16 tells us that God loves us so much that He sent His one and only Son, Jesus, to make forgiveness possible.

2. Do you know what sin is?

    Sin is disobeying God. Sin breaks our friendship with God. Romans 3:23 says, "Everyone has sinned. No one measures up to God's glory." Everyone has disobeyed God. The Bible says in Romans 6:23 the consequence of sin is death, but the gift of God is life forever in Jesus. Jesus saves us from sin and death. That is good news! **Although we do not deserve it, God loves us so much He made a way to fix our broken relationship with Him.** 1 John 4:9 says, "How did God show His love for us? He sent His one and only Son into the world so that we could receive life through Him."

3. Do you know who Jesus is?
    I. Jesus, God's one and only Son, came as a little baby. He grew to be a man that told everyone about God's love and showed people how to love with God's perfect love. He fed hungry people, healed sick people, and made dead people alive again!
    II. Some people did not believe that Jesus was God's son and decided to kill Him. Jesus allowed this to happen to show the world God's great love. God brought Jesus back to life again and showed His power over sin and death!
    III. Jesus is alive today! He loves you and wants to be your Savior and Friend forever. All you need to do is ask God to forgive you for disobeying Him and believe that He will do it. We do not have to stay separated from God! We can accept Jesus' gift of forgiveness and life.

4. Would you like Jesus to be your Savior and best Friend and to begin to live as a child of God?

    It is as easy as A-B-C!

    A: Admit that I have sinned and I need God to forgive me and to help me change.

    B: Believe that God loves me and sent His only Son, Jesus, so I can be forgiven.

    C: Claim Jesus as my Savior and claim my new identity as a child of God.

5. Would you like to pray with me as I pray for you?

   "Dear God, thank You for loving me and sending Jesus to earth. Thank You for allowing Jesus to die for the things that I have done wrong and for raising Him to life again. I am sorry that I have disobeyed You. Please forgive me. I want Jesus to always be with me. Help me to obey You every day. I believe You love me and have forgiven me. Thank You for making me your child. I believe that You will be with me forever! Amen."

   When Jesus is our Savior, He will always be with us. He will help us to live the way that God wants us to live. Romans 12:2 says, "Do not conform to the pattern of this world, but be transformed by the renewing of your mind." Living for God means that we will act differently toward others than we did before. We will want to know His will and do things that please Him. We will want to be kind and loving. We will talk to God in prayer and listen to God in His Word. (This is how we become God's friend.)

Tell the child how excited you are that they are now a child of God. Let them know that you will pray for them. Invite them to come to church. Tell them that it will be important for them to learn more about God through reading the Bible and by talking to Him through prayer. Make sure that you let the child's leader know that the child made a decision to become a Christian so that the people in the church can follow up with this precious new believer and their family.

OPERATION TRANSFORMATION

DAY ONE

DAY ONE

Table of Contents

Leadership Meeting **6**

Opening & Welcome **8**

Opening Skit **10**

Transformation Stations **15**
    Mission Brief 15
    Evidence Vault 19
    Craft Lab 22
    Recharge Station 24
    Agent Training Field 26
    Infiltration Service Project 28

Closing Skit **29**

DAY ONE

Leadership Meeting

- Greeting and appreciation
- Our goal is to *help kids experience life-transforming encounters with Jesus Christ.*
- Review training meeting highlights (bathroom policy, safety policy, discipline, what to do in case of illness or emergency, releasing children at day's end, etc.). Since the details were provided at a prior training, offer these on a single printed page as a reminder.
- Remind leaders of the special offering project.

Day 1 Overview:

Today's Passcode:	Today's Theology Focus:	Today's Bible Story:
Jesus' love transforms my identity!	**Salvation** Use every opportunity to weave this into your time with the kids.	**Acts 9:1-19** (read aloud)

Review Today's Memory Verse:

John 1:12
"Yet to all who did receive him, to those who believed in his name,
he gave the right to become children of God."

Review Top Secret Hand Signal:

Tap-tap, clap-clap, snap-snap, SHHHHHH!

Pat palms on top of legs two times, clap hands two times, snap fingers two times, and place finger to lips while shushing. NOTE: some people have difficulty snapping their fingers; encourage them to close all four fingers onto their palms.

- Review today's songs. Motions to John 1:12 are included on the media section of nazarene.org/vbs.
- Review today's schedule.
- Questions, comments, or concerns?
- Close with prayer at least 15 minutes before start time.

OUR PRAYER FOR YOU:

Father God, we worship You for Who You are.

There is no one like You, Who loves, seeks, and saves the lost.

All of our preparation has brought us to this moment.

Now, Father, bring the children You know need to be here today.

Cut out all distractions so the Good News will go forth without hindrance.

Give us ears to hear Your Spirit and the right words to communicate Your love to the children.

Help us remember what we have prepared to present to the children today.

Give us the energy and enthusiasm to make Your Word

as exciting, engaging, and powerful as it truly is.

We pray the children will fall in love with You and with Your Word.

Draw them by Your grace into a right relationship with you.

Grant us strength to carry out Your work here today.

Protect these kids and these workers.

Take care of our families at home while we seek to expand your Kingdom here.

May Your Kingdom come and Your will be done here today.

We will be careful to give You all the glory.

In Jesus' name and for the sake of His Kingdom,

Amen.

DAY ONE

Opening & Welcome

Be prepared to transition quickly from music to dialogue to music to skit to keep attention focused.

Sing Theme Song with Hand Motions

Starting with music engages everyone's attention and participation.

Welcome

The following is a suggested script:

Director: Welcome to *Operation Transformation!* I am Special Agent _____ and it's so great to see all of you today! I have been looking forward to being on this mission with you. We are going to have a great week! Did you know you have just learned our memory verse for the week? *(Say the verse you just sang.)*

Top Secret Hand Signal

Director: The first thing I need to do is teach you the *Operation Transformation* top secret hand signal. Signals tell us what to do, right? A stop sign signals drivers to do what? *(Pause)*
Correct! It tells them to stop. Our top secret hand signal tells us to stop and listen quietly so everyone can hear what's about to happen. If you have anything in your hands, put it under your chair or the chair in front of you. Your leaders will do it first to show you how it's done. Stand up, leaders! Ready, set, go!

Tap-tap, clap-clap, snap-snap, SHHHHHH!

Alright! Now everybody stand up and let's try it all together when I say "Go." Ready, set, go! *(Pause)*
YES! That was OUTSTANDING! Alright, everybody sit down.

Offering

Director: We are going to do something VERY special this week! We will receive an offering each day. The boys will place their offering here *(Show boys' bucket)* and the girls will place their offering here *(Show girls' bucket)*.

An offering is a gift we give to help God's people share the Good News of Jesus with others. All the money you give this week will help kids around the world to join the mission through the Kids Reaching Kids offering project. *(Explain your mission project. You can find information about the Kids Reaching Kids Offering at nazarene.org/sdmi.)*

With *Operation Transformation*, we are going to MAKE A DIFFERENCE in the lives of girls and boys around the world! Pretty cool, right? In a minute, some special agents are going to teach us our theme song for the week. So when you hear the music begin, follow your leader to bring your offering—and be sure to put it in the right place! Don't worry if you don't have anything to give today; follow your leader anyway. Now that you know, you can bring it tomorrow. We'll all meet back here before you go home and that's when we'll see if the GIRLS or BOYS won!

(Play the theme song and receive the offering. Use this time to make any other special announcements. When everyone has returned to their seats, lead them in the top secret hand signal to get their attention.)

Great job everyone! You just heard the official *Operation Transformation* theme song. We'll be singing it every day—but of course we have to learn it first! So let's meet the special agents leading music this week *(Introduce worship team)*.

Sing Theme Song with Hand Motions

Sing Day 1 Song with Hand Motions

DAY ONE

Opening Skit

Props & Characters:

- **1 box with a lid,** clearly marked "Top Secret" in large red letters with a "thumbprint scanner" (found in the resource section of nazarene.org/vbs) on the lid. This is the special agent lockbox. Feel free to be creative. For instance, placing a battery operated light inside will make the box glow and add mystery to the contents.
- **1 white flower** (preferably a carnation) and an **NIV Bible or New Testament**. These are placed inside the lockbox beforehand. Make note of Acts 9:4-6.
- **1-2 chairs**
- **Small table** with a **clear vase**
- Optional **clipboards** for Tre & Buddy (holding their scripts to access when cues/prompts needed)
- **Special Agent Tre** (Code Name: Trinity); dressed like a spy, with a hat and sunglasses
- **Agent-In-Training Buddy** (Code Name: Barnabas); dressed in street clothes

Note: Use any additional props available to increase interest. Encourage the characters to move often and to use the whole platform/stage.

Dialogue:

Director: Hey everybody! I want to introduce a friend of mine. He's here to recruit our help for a secret mission. The thing is, I don't know his real name because…well, because he's a special agent! His code name is Trinity but I've always called him Tre! So stand up and let's all welcome Special Agent Tre with our top secret hand signal!

Tap-tap, clap-clap, snap-snap, shhhhhh!

(Tre strides confidently onstage.)

Agent Tre: Wow! I'm not used to all this attention. Thank you for that wonderful welcome! That reminds me of a song…

(Starts shouting/singing) "Yet to all who did receive him…"

(Interrupting himself) Hey! That song goes perfectly with today's secret passcode. I'd love to share it with you but I can't…unless…

(Ponders for a moment) …unless you all became official *Operation Transformation* recruits.

Then I could tell you the passcode AND you could help me with my mission! Sound like a good idea? OK! Everybody who wants to be an official recruit stand up. Let's start with the top secret hand signal. Ready?

Tap-tap, clap-clap, snap-snap, shhhhhh!

OK, raise your right hand *(Raises right hand shoulder-high)*.

By the power vested in me, I hereby appoint you official *Operation Transformation* recruits. Great! Have a seat.

Here's today's secret passcode: **Jesus' love transforms my identity!**

Got it? Let's say it together: **Jesus' love transforms my identity!**

Now just the girls: **Jesus' love transforms my identity!**

And now just the boys! **Jesus' love transforms my identity!**

Now all together: **Jesus' love transforms my identity!**

What a great group of recruits! Thanks, Special Agent _____!

(Director walks offstage)

> Buddy: *(Stumbles in from offstage and faces Tre, oblivious to the crowd)* There you are!

Agent Tre: *(Very serious)* Passcode?

> Buddy: Oh, right.

(Stands at attention and says loudly) **Jesus' love transforms my identity!** Sorry I'm late, Tre. I wasn't sure if this was the right place. You said we were having a secret meeting here but when I saw all the cars, I thought I must be in the wrong place because I didn't see how we could hold a secret meeting with all these people around. But I decided to look anyway and I'm glad I did, because here you are! And…

(Looks around as if seeing the kids for the first time; drops his voice to an exaggerated whisper) Here they are! Oh man! I hope they didn't just hear everything I said…because then our secret meeting wouldn't be a secret…I guess there's only one way to find out.

(Faces the kids, speaking in full voice) Excuse me; excuse me—did anybody happen to hear anything I just said to Tre?

(Expect kids to holler "yes, we heard you;" "no, we didn't hear you;" etc.)

OH NO! I am SO sorry Tre; I've ruined *everything*! Sharing secret information in front of strangers. Now I'll never become a special agent! *(Head in hands, Buddy collapses into a pitiful puddle)*

Agent Tre: Hold on a minute. These aren't strangers; they're just new friends you haven't met! *(Turns to audience)* Am I right, kids? Recruits, this is Agent-In-Training Code Name Barnabas—but you can call him Buddy. Everybody, say hello to Buddy. *(Turns to Buddy and gestures to the audience)*

Buddy, *these* are the new recruits I was telling you about! They're going to help us with *Operation Transformation*. And some of them might even become agents-in-training like you. And if you think there are a lot of them here today, just wait 'til they've had a chance to tell all their friends about *Operation Transformation!*

Buddy: That's awesome, Tre! It seems like only yesterday that I was a brand new recruit just like them.

(Suddenly fearful) Have you told them about Deceptor, yet? What if *he* shows up?

Agent Tre: Don't worry about Deceptor, Buddy. I have a plan to deal with him. Now, where was I? Oh… right! I was getting ready to show these recruits the latest piece of equipment from Headquarters. It's a special agent lockbox.

(Tre pulls the box to center stage and makes a big deal of "scanning" his thumbprint on the scanner. He opens the top and begins to insert his hand when Buddy interrupts.)

Buddy: Whoa! Wait a minute! Did I just see what I thought I saw? Please tell me you didn't just scan your thumbprint to unlock that box!

Agent Tre: Well, as a matter of fact, I did. *(Closes the box again without removing contents)*

Buddy: AWESOME! That is so cool! Can I try it?

Agent Tre: OK…but you won't be able to… *(Chuckles to himself and looks knowingly at the kids as Buddy "scans" his thumbprint)*

Buddy: *(Buddy tries to open the box but can't. He huffs and puffs, gets frustrated, tries repeatedly, seems to pull even harder on the lid as if it's been nailed shut. Buddy can really play this up like he's giving it ALL he's got to open the box but to no avail.)*

What is WRONG with this BOX? You need to take it back to Headquarters, Tre. It's obviously not working right. Unless I broke it. Did I break it? Oh no! I can't believe I broke it! I am SO sorry, Tre! I wasn't trying to break it. You saw me, right? I scanned my thumbprint, just like you, but the lid wouldn't budge!

Agent Tre: You didn't break it, Buddy. It can only be opened by the special agent it's assigned to. That's what makes this scanner so awesome! If it was locked with a key, or a combination, or even a password, anybody who found the key, combination, or password could open it. But no two people on the entire planet have the same fingerprints—not even identical twins! That's how God made us and *that's* why I'm the only one who can open *this* lockbox! *(Scans his thumbprint, easily opens the box, and removes a white carnation and NIV Bible)*

Buddy: THAT/IS/SO/COOL!!! You know, I'm grateful to be an agent-in-training because I'm learning so much, but I cannot WAIT to become a special agent like you. When will that happen, Tre?

Agent Tre: Well, it's different for everyone, Buddy. Both of my parents were special agents and as long as I can remember, that's all I ever wanted to be. *(Tre puts down the flower but holds on to the Bible)*

But that's not how it is for everybody. For example, take the story of Special Agent Paul written in the Handbook. His transformation was so radical that he changed his name from Saul to Paul. As you know, the Bible is the Official *Operation Transformation* Agent Handbook. You can find the beginning of Paul's story in the book of Acts.

Paul grew up in a very religious family who named him Saul and taught him that the only way to please God was to carefully follow all of the religious rules. And that's what he did. So when he grew up, he would get very angry with anybody who said that following Jesus was the only way to please God. He hated anyone who had anything good to say about Jesus.

Buddy: But wait…I'm confused. I thought you said he was trying to please God.

Agent Tre: He was, but he was deceived by you-know-who.

Buddy: Deceptor?

Agent Tre: Yes sir! Deceptor convinced Saul that he was pleasing God by attacking Christians! Then the strangest thing happened! He was on his way to Damascus to arrest a bunch of Christians when a bright light came out of nowhere and blinded him. It says it right here in the Handbook, in Acts chapter 9, verses 4-6.

(Reads from Bible taken out of lockbox): He fell to the ground and heard a voice say to him, "Saul, Saul, why do you persecute me?" "Who are you, Lord?" Saul asked. "I am Jesus, whom you are persecuting," he replied. "Now get up and go into the city, and you will be told what you must do." *(Close the Bible and set it back on the table)*

In case you don't know, to persecute means to badly mistreat an innocent person or a group of people, usually for a long time.

Buddy: Man! That IS dramatic. So, did the bright light and voice turn him into a special agent?

Agent Tre: Oh, no. They just got his attention. Like everybody who becomes a special agent, he had to confess his sins, believe that Jesus was God's son who died for his sins, claim Jesus as his Savior, and receive God's forgiveness. He was even baptized to show everyone that he was following Jesus, just like those he used to bully!

He was one of the original *Operation Transformation* special agents. He actually wrote several sections of the Special Agent Handbook.

Buddy: Wow! Headed the wrong way…totally convinced he was going in the right direction…bright light…voice from heaven. He did a total 180…new life, new mission, new everything! That's a lot to take in.

Agent Tre: Yes it is! But as you know, Buddy, the more you learn about *Operation Transformation*, the more it all starts to make sense. Oh! Oh! *(Starts laughing and hopping on one foot)* Hang on. Someone's calling me on my special agent shoe phone! *(Takes off his shoe and sticks it to his head like a phone)*

Buddy: *(Looking at the kids)* Phone? I didn't hear a phone; did you hear a phone?

Agent Tre: *(Covers the "phone" and whispers to Buddy)* It's silent of course…but when it vibrates it really tickles!

(Now talking on the phone) "Hello, this is Tre. Excuse me? The passcode? Oh, right, **Jesus' love transforms my identity!** Sorry sir; yes sir. I'll leave right away, sir. Thank you, sir." *(Pushes something on the shoe to "hang up the call" and puts it back on his foot)*

I'm sorry, Buddy, we'll have to finish our meeting later. The Boss just gave me a new assignment and I have to leave right away. *(Starts walking offstage)*

Buddy: Wait! What about the flower?

Agent Tre: *(Keeps walking offstage)* The kids will learn about it in their Mission Brief.

Buddy: Can I go with you?

Agent Tre: If you hustle!

Buddy: *(Running after him)* Hold on, I'm coming! Bye, kids!

(Director walks onstage)

Director: I wonder what's so special about that white flower? Oh well, Tre said we'll find out in the Mission Brief. So everybody follow your team leaders to your first activity and I'll see you back here at the end of the day to share what we learn about that flower and to find out about the offering!

Closing:

If time allows, sing 1-2 songs focused on salvation, God's love, and Jesus our Savior.

End with Day 1 Song, *"John 1:12, Yet to all who did receive him,"* with hand motions.

Kids are dismissed by groups and given any instructions they need to get to their Transformation Station.

Play theme song as children exit.

DAY ONE

Transformation Station

MISSION BRIEF: FLOWER POWER

Conduct an experiment to show how accepting Jesus' love, reading God's Word, and spending time with God's people transforms us to be like Christ.

Preparation:

- If possible, the leader should wear a **white lab coat**.
- Prepare a **large manila envelope** with "MISSION BRIEF #1" written in large letters on the outside. Place a copy of the **script** inside.
- Gather flower transformation experiment materials: **white flower, clear vase or glass, water, red food coloring, knife or scissors.**
- Have a current **NIV Bible** with your supplies.

Directions:

View the links below and choose an experiment to conduct with the children. Practice your experiment at home one week prior to VBS. The longer the flower sits in colorful water, the more colorful the flower becomes. This provides an example of continuing transformation over time.

Take a picture immediately after placing the white flower in the red water. If possible print the picture and place where the group will be able to see it tomorrow. Each day we will take a picture and track the changes in the flower.

Options:

- kidzone.ws/science/carnations.htm
- littlepassports.com/blog/craft-diy/carnation-science-experiment
- msichicago.org/experiment/hands-on-science/color-changing-carnations

Mission Brief Summary:

1. Retell Saul's story (Jesus' love transformed Saul's identity).
2. Explain the flower analogy.
3. Invite them into a transformational relationship with Jesus.

Mission Brief Leader Suggested Script:

(Feel free to adapt to your context.)

Come on in!

Who remembers what Special Agent Tre pulled out of his secret lockbox? *(Pause for answers)*
Right! A Bible and a flower.

What color was the flower? *(Pause for answers)*
Right again! That white flower is a clue to an important message for us in today's mission briefing.

(Remove this script from a manila envelope with "MISSION BRIEF #1" written in large letters on the outside and begin reading.)

The story begins with a man named Saul traveling to a city called Damascus. On his way to Damascus, Saul was blinded by a very bright light.

Why was Saul going to Damascus? *(Pause for answers)*
Right! He was going to arrest all the Christians and take them back to Jerusalem as prisoners.

The men traveling with Saul heard a loud voice speaking to him, but they didn't see anyone talking. Whose voice did they hear speaking to Saul? *(Pause for answers)*
Jesus!

Jesus told Saul to enter the city, but Saul needed the others to help him get there. Why did Saul need help walking to Damascus? *(Pause for answers)*
Because he was blinded by the bright light and couldn't see where he was going.

Why is walking risky when you can't see where you're going? *(Pause for answers)*
Right! Because you can hurt yourself if you trip or bump into something.

(Follow the script or open the Bible and use the Handbook to continue the story of Saul starting at Acts 9:9.)

After Saul made it to Damascus, Jesus gave Special Agent Ananias an important mission that would require great courage. Jesus told Ananias, "Go to the house of Judas on Straight Street and ask for a man from Tarsus named Saul, for he is praying. In a vision he has seen a man named Ananias come and place his hands on him to restore his sight" (Acts 9:11-12).

Why would Agent Ananias need great courage to complete the mission? *(Pause for answers)* Because he was one of the Christians that Saul was coming to Damascus to arrest!

Ananias was scared and he said to Jesus, "I have heard many reports about this man and all the harm he has done to your saints in Jerusalem. And he has come here with authority from the chief priests to arrest all who call on your name" (Acts 9:13-14).

Ananias didn't know that Saul already had an amazing encounter with Jesus on his way to Damascus. So Ananias thought Saul was still a very dangerous threat, not only to him but to all of God's special agents in Damascus. Ananias didn't know that Jesus was preparing Saul for a very special mission: to travel to many different places, telling everyone that Jesus was the Son of God who could forgive sins and transform everyone who believed into a precious child of God!

Jesus didn't argue with Ananias. He simply said, "Go! This man is my chosen instrument to carry my name…" (Acts 9:15).

So, Ananias did what all good agents do: He obeyed Jesus! Even though Ananias was afraid, he knew that Jesus loved him and would never abandon him, no matter what. So Ananias went to the house on Straight Street, placed his hands on Saul and said, "Brother Saul, the Lord—Jesus, who appeared to you on the road as you were coming here—has sent me so that you may see again and be filled with the Holy Spirit." Immediately…he could see again. He got up and was baptized, and after taking some food, he regained his strength (Acts 9:17-19).

So, what does that story have to do with this? *(Hold the flower up)* We're going to use this white flower to show what happens when we choose to follow Jesus and accept Him as our Savior! *(Place the flower in the vase with colored water)*

During the week, we will see this flower transform! That's why it's such a great clue. It reminds us that God wants to transform all of us into His special agents.

We can become God's special agents if we confess our sins and believe that:
- God loves us and sent his Son, Jesus, to save the world.
- Jesus died on the cross so our sins could be forgiven.
- Jesus rose from the dead and He is alive today.

Believing these things and receiving Jesus as our Savior will transform us! We will be "born again" and adopted into God's family! As precious sons and daughters of God, we receive a new identity!

When God transforms us, it changes everything! We feel His love on the inside, and that changes what we want do on the outside. We can stop saying and doing bad things because we are transformed into children of God. We actually *want* to please God, and we finally have the power to do just that! As God's special agents, we pay close attention to our choices and our actions, like what we watch, what we read, what we listen to, and even what we think about!

The Bible is God's Word. That makes it the ultimate Special Agent Handbook! Some parts of it were even written by Saul after he became Special Agent Paul. Here's what Paul said in a letter he wrote to the special agents in Rome: "Do not conform any longer to the pattern of this world, but be transformed by the renewing of your mind." And the verse goes on to say, "Then you will be able to test and approve what God's will is—his good, pleasing, and perfect will" (Romans 12:2a).

Transformation is our mission. To help us accomplish the mission, let's memorize this verse over the next few days. Let's start by repeating the verse. *(Repeat the verse with motions; play the Operation Transformation theme song and sing along.)*

This flower represents our lives being transformed by the renewing of our minds. The flower must connect to water to live. The flower's transformation begins when the flower is placed in the red water instead of the normal, everyday water. For our life to be transformed, we must connect to God. The problem is that our sin separates us from God, and only God can restore that connection. We cannot transform ourselves. The good news is that God provided a way for us to connect with Him and be transformed through his Son, Jesus. That is why it is so important for us to receive Jesus as our Savior. It is as easy as A-B-C!

A: Admit that I have sinned and I need God to forgive me and to help me change.

B: Believe that God loves me and sent His only Son, Jesus, so I can be forgiven.

C: Claim Jesus as my Savior and claim my new identity as a child of God.

When we do this, we connect to God in a powerful way, and He transforms us. God helps us live a life that pleases Him and share His love with others. God's Word is important to our transformation. When we memorize God's Word, we take God's transforming power with us wherever we go. Then, whenever we need help, God can speak truth to us through His powerful, transforming Word.

If any of you want to be transformed into God's special agent, like Paul, just tell me or one of your leaders and we will pray with you about receiving Jesus as your Savior. OK? OK! Let's all say today's special agent passcode: **Jesus' love transforms my identity!** Tomorrow we will see what happened to our flower overnight!

DAY ONE

Transformation Station

**EVIDENCE VAULT:
JOHN 1:12**

Play the theme song or memory verse song as children enter the room. Open your time with the top secret hand signal.

Supplies:

- Recording of the day's **memory verse song**
- A wrapped **gift with a name tag**
- **Memory verse chart**
- Optional **prizes or mission money**
- **Supplies for memory verse game** from the resource section of nazarene.org/vbs

Evidence Vault Leader Suggested Script:

Who remembers today's secret passcode? *(Pause for answers)*
Jesus' love transforms my identity!

Our verse today helps us better understand the passcode. Our verse is:

John 1:12
"Yet to all who did receive him, to those who believed in his name, he gave the right to become children of God."

What does this verse mean?

When you receive a present with your name on it for Christmas or your birthday, what do you do with it? *(Open it; pause for answers)*
Right! You accept the gift, open it, and thank the person who gave it to you. That is what this verse is talking about!

The Bible says God is love. God loves all people so much He sent His son, Jesus, to earth to live with us and show us how to love like God loves. Jesus is God's greatest gift to the world. Through believing in Jesus, He gives us the right to become children of God! Jesus is an incredible gift from God to you and to me! He is a gift of love with our names on it! God's love is powerful!

What would happen if someone gave you a present but you didn't know about it or didn't believe it was yours and so you never opened it? Would you be able to really enjoy it if you never accepted it or opened it?

That's what this verse is saying! If I accept God's love for me and believe in Jesus as my Savior, God's powerful love transforms me and I become a precious child of God. I am no longer just __*(your name)*__! Jesus' love has transformed my identity into __*(your name)*__, a precious child of God!

If you wonder how to accept the gift of Jesus, talk to me or your leader and we will pray with you.

This is good news! That is why today's memory verse is so important to learn. What's our passcode? *(Pause for answers)*
Jesus' love transforms my identity!

We want to be able to share this good news with others by learning our memory verse.

(Be prepared to say the verse with a rhythm or sing it with the motions. Have fun. Teach the verse a few words at a time modeling the motions slowly. Include the reference. Talk about how the motions reflect the words in the verse. After you have said it a couple of times, speed it up. Play and sing along with the memory verse song for the day.)

Let's say today's memory verse. Repeat after me:
**Yet to all who did receive him,
to those who believed in his name,
he gave the right to become
children of God.
John 1:12**

One more time:
**Yet to all who did receive him,
to those who believed in his name,
he gave the right to become
children of God.
John 1:12**

Here's an exciting thought: the verses you memorize this week will be with you the rest of your life! Memorize this verse and you will always be able to tell someone else that they, too, can become a precious child of God.

Closing:

Outline the plan your church has made to reward children that memorize Scripture this week. A downloadable memory verse chart is provided for you to write the children's names and keep track of who has memorized which verses. Allow them time each day to repeat them to you.

Go over the memory verse several times.

If they are ready, have children come to you individually to say their verse. Mark it on the memory verse chart. If you are giving prizes or secret mission money for saying today's portion of the verse, hand them out now.

If time allows, play a memory verse game from the memory verse games resource.

DAY ONE

Transformation Station

CRAFT LAB: IDENTITY BADGE

Play the theme song and the memory verse song as children arrive. Ask the children to repeat the memory verse or the passcode for the day.

Supplies:
- **Name tag** (found in the resource section of nazarene.org/vbs)
- **Paper**
- **Stamp pad**
- **Magnifying glass**
- **Crayons, markers, or colored pencils**

Directions:
Have each child use a stamp pad to put their thumbprint on one piece of paper so that the paper contains the thumbprints of every child. Use the magnifying glass to see the thumbprints clearly. Discuss how each thumbprint is completely different.

Craft Lab Leader Suggested Script:
When you checked in, they gave you a nametag. Today we are going to transform our nametags into identity badges.

God made each of us unique. No two persons have the same thumbprints. That is why police departments and security agencies use fingerprints to identify people. Add your thumbprint to your special agent identification badge. Your thumbprint belongs only to you.

Turn the identification badge over. Draw a picture of yourself. Try to make it look as much like you as possible.

Remember today's skit? Tre used his thumbprint to open the top secret lockbox, but Buddy's thumbprint did NOT open the box. Why do you think he couldn't open the box? *(Pause for answers)*
Because he did not have access! The box would only open if it recognized Tre's identity by his thumbprint.

When you are born, the hospital may record your handprints and footprints to officially identify you. You have the same thumbprint all of your life. If you become a Christian and receive new life in Jesus, does that change your thumbprint? *(Pause for answers)*
NO!

Do you look different on the outside? *(Pause for answers)*
NO!

When you accept Jesus as your Savior and God's love transforms you, what changes—the inside or the outside? *(Pause for answers)*
Right! He changes us on the inside.

Because God transforms your heart, you want to please God in your daily life and *that* changes what we *do* on the outside.

We have a Helper and a Friend to guide us. Just like Tre's thumbprint gave him access to open the lockbox, becoming a Christian gives us access to the greatest treasure in the universe: God Himself! We can ask Him questions and He hears us. He gives us a clean heart. He gives us wisdom when we ask Him. He is with us when we are hurting and helps us overcome the lies of Deceptor, who tempts us to disobey. God protects us by warning us when we are in danger. Giving our lives to Jesus gives us access to all kinds of amazing things!

Closing:

If time allows, share your testimony. How did God change your life? Did He take away resentments and give you a heart of compassion? Did He wash away your guilty conscience and give you joy and freedom from shame? Let the Lord lead the discussion at the age level of the kids in the room. Allow them to ask questions if they wish. If there is additional time, allow children to share what they learned today.

DAY ONE

Transformation Station

RECHARGE STATION: ROAD TO DAMASCUS

Play the theme song and the memory verse song as children arrive. Ask the children to repeat the memory verse or passcode for the day.

Supplies:
- **Graham crackers**
- **Yellow icing**
- **Crystal sprinkles**
- **Pretzel sticks**
- **Plastic spoons**
- **Napkins**

Directions:
Give each child one full graham cracker along with a spoonful of icing that has already been colored yellow. Have the children spread the icing on the cracker and use the sprinkles on top of the "road." Use the pretzel sticks to outline the road. Discuss God's transformation of Saul in **Acts 9:1-19**.

Recharge Station Leader Suggested Script:
Today we're going to make a road or pathway with our snacks. We want to remember that Paul started down the road believing the wrong things before he met Jesus that day and his life was transformed. We want to think about our own life while we are decorating our snack.

The most important thing in the whole world is that we experience God's transforming love and have a relationship with Him through Jesus.

Isn't it incredible that God stopped Saul on the road that day so Saul could hear Jesus' voice and know God's powerful, transforming love? Does God always use a bright light to show Himself to people? *(Pause for answers)*
NO!

What other ways does God use to show Himself to people? *(Pause for answers)*
Through nature, He shows He is Creator. Through the Bible He reveals Who He is. Through His people and His Church, He shows His love. He talks to us in our hearts, and we just know that He is real.

How does God show us His love?

The Bible says we all are heading the wrong way. We all are on the wrong path until we meet Jesus, receive His transforming love, and choose to follow Him and take His direction, like Saul. Experiencing the powerful transforming love of Jesus and following Him is sweet, just like the icing and the things we are using to decorate our snack today are transforming our snack into something good and yummy!

What if someone has met Jesus today, like Saul? Or maybe they heard the lessons here at VBS and someone wants to know more about Him? Where can they find out more about Jesus to get to know Him and his transforming love better? *(Pause for answers)*
Read the Bible, learn from other people who know Him, go to Church where they teach us about Him, pray to Him.

Always remember what you have learned today and how God's transforming love is powerful and sweet. Just like with Paul, Jesus will transform your identity into a child of God and give you a new start on a good path, if you follow Him.

DAY ONE

Transformation Station

AGENT TRAINING FIELD: HOLD ON, SAUL! (STATUES GAME)

Equipment:
None

Set Up:
Mark a line on the ground or pavement. Mark another line a good distance away from the first. Select a child to be "It." The players stand on one line; "It" stands on the other line.

Objective:
To see which player can reach the other side first.

How to Play the Game:
The player who is "It" turns his/her back to the others and counts aloud to ten.

As "It" counts, the other players walk as fast as they can toward the other line.

At the count of ten, "It" whirls around and says, "HOLD ON, SAUL!" and all the players freeze into statues. Any player caught moving must go back to the starting line.

"It" can say "You need a new start! Let's try my way!" to anyone who gets caught moving. Then "It" can tell the players that were "caught" to move in a different way next time: "hop on one foot," "take baby steps," "crawl on your hands and knees," "next time take only one step or a sideways step," etc.

The one who is "It" can count as slowly or quickly as he/she wants. This goes on until one player crosses the line and wins the game. The new winner is now "It" and the game starts again.

Memory Verse Application:

(After you have played several times) How is this game like our story about Saul? *(Pause for answers)* Saul was stopped on his way. Saul was told to wait. Saul was given another chance to follow Jesus. Saul began a new direction. Saul had to follow the directions.

Saul was heading in the wrong direction in his life. Saul did not know that Jesus really was God's Son and the Savior. When Jesus spoke to Saul in the bright light, he was saying, "Hold on, Saul! You are going the wrong way and you need a brand new start! Let's try my way!"

Optional Game: Blind Man's Path

Create a pathway (or several if space allows) by marking lines on the floor with tape. Place items on the path as obstacles for children to walk around as they move down the path.

Divide children in pairs and provide a blindfold to one child in each pair. Tell them that the goal is to reach the end of the path without hitting an obstacle.

Ask the child who can see to verbally guide the blindfolded child around obstacles to reach the end of the path. Have the children trade places. Then discuss these questions:

1. How did it feel to not be able to see? *(Pause for answers)*
   Scary, hard.
2. What did you do to get to the end of the path? *(Pause for answers)*
   Listen for instructions, walk slowly, wait until someone told me what to do.
3. How do you think Saul felt when he was blind? *(Pause for answers)*

Saul had gotten off the right path and was persecuting Christians. He needed the help of God and others to put him on the right path and receive a new identity. Let's pray and thank God for His guidance and love.

DAY ONE

Transformation Station

INFILTRATION SERVICE PROJECT

Work on something or give something that reflects Jesus offering us new life through the power of His transforming love.

Remember:

The importance of this activity is to teach the children the value of reaching out to others, so no matter which activity you choose, point to the fact that this gift represents new life through Jesus.

Write a note to deliver with each gift that says, "At VBS this week, we are learning that Jesus' love transforms our identity and gives us a new life. May God bless your with the power of His transforming love!" Have the children sign it.

Ideas:

- Plant flowers in little pots to give to house-bound people at your church (can be from seed, can be taking already growing flowers in flats and separating in smaller pots as gifts).
- Assemble gift baskets for the new parents in your church or for a local organization that helps single moms. Provide church members a list of items to donate for this project. Gather donated items ahead of time. Items could include diapers, wipes, baby soaps, baby washcloths, etc.
- Plant flowers or even vegetables in a garden plot or in pots. Tell the children "We are planting these now so that we can bless others with the beauty or food that grows from this new life!"

DAY ONE

Closing Skit

Play theme song and memory verse song as children return.

Ask volunteers to share the passcode, memory verse, favorite activity, or something they learned. Or have trivia questions prepared to ask early arrivers.

Begin with the top secret hand signal.

Dialogue:

Director: What a great day we had learning that **Jesus' love transforms my identity!** Let's welcome back our worship leader to review our two songs for today.

(Worship leader sings theme song and today's memory verse song with hand motions.)

(Buddy and Tre walk on stage. Buddy clumsily trips.)

    Buddy: Agent Tre, THAT WAS AWESOME! Thanks for letting me ride along. It must feel great to go around helping people all the time.

Agent Tre: Being a part of *Operation Transformation* is great, Buddy. It's not always easy, but it IS always rewarding because what we do changes lives.

    Buddy: How did you know what to say to that lady you helped?

Agent Tre: In addition to my special agent shoe phone, every special agent has a built-in receiver tuned to the Boss's frequency that allows Him to speak directly to each one of us. The thing is, it's not very loud so I have to listen very carefully. That's why it helps to memorize as much of the Handbook as possible. That way, I've always got it in here *(Taps his head)*, because much of what He says comes out of here *(Holds up a Bible)*.

    Buddy: Are you saying the Boss wrote the Agent Handbook? I thought you said Paul wrote it.

Agent Tre: Paul wrote part of it. God also spoke through many other writers over the years. The important thing to remember is that God inspired the words they wrote. So even though different writers wrote different parts at different times, everything in the Handbook tells about God's love for us. It's really the story of God's love for the world. Everything in it points us to God's love and prepares the way for *Operation Transformation*. That's what makes this such an exciting time to be a special agent.

    Buddy: How did we get in this mess to begin with, Tre? Why do we even need *Operation Transformation*?

Agent Tre: That's a great question, Buddy. In the beginning, everything was good. God created the world and then He created us in His image, as His children. He put us in charge of a world filled with His presence, beauty, and love. We lived in loving relationship with God and each other, secure in our identity as precious children of light.

Buddy: Well, that's sure not how it is now! What happened?

Agent Tre: What happened is that Deceptor showed up!

Buddy: Do you mean the devil?

Agent Tre: He goes by a lot of names, Buddy. Satan, Lucifer, the devil, Deceptor. He's sneaky and evil, he hates God, and he hates us too! He lied to Adam and Eve. He persuaded them to disobey God and when they did, everything changed. They hid from God because they felt ashamed, and they felt ashamed because they had sinned. They traded their identity as children of light for a terrible identity as children of darkness. That's why disobedience is the root of all sin.

Buddy: I'm glad I don't sin!

Agent Tre: Are you sure, Buddy? Have you ever told a lie?

Buddy: Uh, yeah, but not very big ones.

Agent Tre: Have you ever disobeyed your parents or taken something that didn't belong to you? Have you ever said or done something mean to hurt someone else because you were mad at them?

Buddy: Well… *(Head hanging down)* …yes. Yes. Yes and yes.

Agent Tre: *(Holding the Bible up)* The Handbook calls all of those things sin.

Buddy: Well, then I guess I have sinned after all. *(Scratching his head)*

Agent Tre: Buddy, everyone has sinned. Every. Single. Person. Even me. Even Special Agent Paul. But I have some Good News for you. Actually, it's great news! God wasn't happy about Deceptor tricking Adam and Eve into disobeying Him. So God did something incredible! He came into the world as a baby, just like us.

Buddy: Are you talking about Jesus?

Agent Tre: Exactly! Jesus became like us so we could become like Him! When Jesus grew up, Deceptor tempted Him, just like he tempts each of us. But his tricks didn't work on Jesus. Jesus resisted those temptations and won the battle over sin, and shame, and even Deceptor himself! And when He died and rose again, He was even victorious over death.

Buddy: Are you talking about Jesus dying on the cross?

Agent Tre: Yes! Jesus died on the cross for our sins, but He rose again and He's alive today. Jesus died for us so we could live for Him! If we accept His sacrifice, our sins are forgiven and we receive a new identity. We're transformed by God's love from children of darkness into children of light.

  Buddy: Oh, now I get it! That's *Operation Transformation!*

Agent Tre: Right. Jesus launched *Operation Transformation* because we couldn't transform ourselves. When we pray and ask Jesus into our hearts, it's HIS power that transforms us.

  Buddy: I sure could use that kind of power. Can I ask Jesus to transform my heart?

Agent Tre: Sure, Buddy! It's as easy as A-B-C!

A: Admit (tell God) that you have disobeyed God.
B: Believe God loves you and sent His son, Jesus, to make it possible for you to be forgiven. Ask for and receive God's forgiveness.
C: Claim Jesus as your Savior and best Friend and claim your new identity as a precious child of God.

  Buddy: I know my ABC's, but would you help me to pray about this right now?

Agent Tre: Sure! *(Turn to the kids)* I know you have learned a lot about the power of God's transforming love today. If you would like to ask God to transform your life, you can pray your own prayer or you can pray this prayer with me and Buddy. Would you bow your heads and close your eyes while we pray?

Dear God, Thank you for sending Jesus to die on the cross for the wrong things I have done. *(Pause while Buddy repeats)*

I admit I have disobeyed you and I am sorry. Please forgive me. *(Pause while Buddy repeats)*

I want Jesus to be my Savior and best friend. *(Pause while Buddy repeats)*

Thank You for forgiving me and giving me a new identity. *(Pause while Buddy repeats)*

Transform me with Your loving power so I can obey You everyday. *(Pause while Buddy repeats)*

In Jesus' name, AMEN!

  Buddy: Thanks, TRE! I can't wait to share this good news!

Agent Tre: Congratulations, Buddy! You are now an official special agent! I was going to give my report on today's mission to the Boss. Why don't you come with me and we can tell the Boss together?

  Buddy: Great! Bye, kids!

Director: Thanks, Buddy and Tre! See you tomorrow! Kids, if you accepted Jesus as your Savior today, your identity is transformed! You are a precious child of God! Please share this news with your leader before you leave today.

God has given us a great first day at *Operation Transformation,* and we have even more to celebrate! While you were in your transformation stations, we counted the offering. Do you want to know who gave the most today, the girls or the boys?

The girls gave $_____ and the boys gave $_____! So who gave the most? *(Pause for answers)* Right! But working together, you gave $_____ to the real winners: children all around the world who will hear about *Operation Transformation* because of your generosity. Way to go!

Everyone, please stand for our closing prayer: Thank You, God, for your transforming love for each one of us and for the generosity of these children. We pray that you will help other children know You and Your Son, Jesus! Amen.

Everyone take off your nametags and give them to your group leader. You can pick them up when you come back tomorrow. OK? And everybody remember to bring a friend, so they can hear about *Operation Transformation* too!

Closing:
Give any other announcements or direction for dismissal. Play theme song as children leave.

OPERATION TRANSFORMATION

DAY TWO

DAY TWO

Table of Contents

Week at a Glance 4

Leadership Meeting 6

Opening & Welcome 8

Opening Skit 10

Transformation Stations 14
    Mission Brief 14
    Evidence Vault 17
    Craft Lab 20
    Recharge Station 21
    Agent Training Field 23
    Infiltration Service Project 25

Closing Skit 26

DAY TWO

Leadership Meeting

- Greeting and appreciation
- Our goal is to *help kids experience life-transforming encounters with Jesus Christ.*
- Review training meeting highlights (bathroom policy, safety policy, discipline, what to do in case of illness or emergency, releasing children at day's end, etc.). Since the details were provided at a prior training, offer these on a single printed page as a reminder.
- Remind leaders of the special offering project.

Day 2 Overview:

Today's Passcode:	Today's Theology Focus:	Today's Bible Story:
Jesus' power transforms my life!	**Initial Sanctification** Use every opportunity to weave this into your time with the kids.	Acts 9:20-30 (read aloud)

Review Today's Memory Verse:

John 10:27
"My sheep listen to my voice; I know them, and they follow me."

Review Top Secret Hand Signal:

Tap-tap, clap-clap, snap-snap, SHHHHHH!

Pat palms on top of legs two times, clap hands two times, snap fingers two times, and place finger to lips while shushing. NOTE: some people have difficulty snapping their fingers; encourage them to close all four fingers onto their palms.

- Review today's songs. Motions to John 10:27 are included on the media section of nazarene.org/vbs.
- Review today's schedule.
- Questions, comments, or concerns?
- Close with prayer at least 15 minutes before start time.

OUR PRAYER FOR YOU:

Father God, we worship You for Who You are.

There is no one like You, Who loves, seeks, and saves the lost.

All of our preparation has brought us to this moment.

Now, Father, bring the children You know need to be here today.

Cut out all distractions so the Good News will go forth without hindrance.

Give us ears to hear Your Spirit and the right words to communicate Your love to the children.

Help us remember what we have prepared to present to the children today.

Give us the energy and enthusiasm to make Your Word

as exciting, engaging, and powerful as it truly is.

We pray the children will fall in love with You and with Your Word.

Draw them by Your grace into a right relationship with you.

Grant us strength to carry out Your work here today.

Protect these kids and these workers.

Take care of our families at home while we seek to expand your Kingdom here.

May Your Kingdom come and Your will be done here today.

We will be careful to give You all the glory.

In Jesus' name and for the sake of His Kingdom,

Amen.

DAY TWO

Opening & Welcome

Be prepared to transition quickly from music to dialogue to music to skit to keep attention focused.

Sing Theme Song and Day 1 Song with Hand Motions

Starting with music engages everyone's attention and participation.

Welcome

The following is a suggested script:

Director: Welcome to Day Two of *Operation Transformation!* I am Special Agent _____ and it's great to see you again! It looks like we have some new friends with us today, so let's teach them our *Operation Transformation* top secret hand signal. This signal tells us to stop, look, and listen. If you have anything in your hands, put it under your chair or the chair in front of you. Leaders first! Stand up, leaders! Ready, set, go!

Tap-tap, clap-clap, snap-snap, SHHHHHH!

Alright! Now everybody stand up and let's try it all together when I say, "Go." Ready, set, go! *(Pause)*
YES! That was OUTSTANDING! All right, everybody sit down.

Offering

Director: We are doing something VERY special this week! We are receiving an offering each day to help God's people share the Good News of Jesus with others. All the money you give this week will help kids everywhere join the mission through the Kids Reaching Kids offering project. *(Explain your mission project. You can find information about the Kids Reaching Kids Offering at nazarene.org/sdmi.)*

Through *Operation Transformation*, we are going to MAKE A DIFFERENCE in the lives of girls and boys around the world! Pretty cool, right? In a minute, some special agents are going to teach us our theme song for the week. So when you hear the music begin, follow your leader to bring your offering—and be sure to put it in the right place! If you don't have anything to give today, follow your leader anyway and be sure to bring it tomorrow. We'll all meet back here before we go home and we'll find out then who gave the most: the GIRLS or the BOYS!

(Play the theme song and receive the offering. Use this time to make any other special announcements. When everyone has returned to their seats, lead them in the top secret hand signal to get their attention.)

Great job everyone! That was the official *Operation Transformation* theme song. Our new friends didn't get a chance to learn it yet, so let's help them out. Everybody please welcome our special agent worship team!

Sing Theme Song with Hand Motions

Sing Day 2 Song with Hand Motions

DAY TWO

Opening Skit

Props & Characters:

- **Special agent lockbox**
- **Butterfly picture** (found in the resource section of nazarene.org/vbs). This is placed in the lockbox with an NIV Bible beforehand.
- **1-2 chairs**
- **1 large magnifying glass**
- **1 large envelope**, marked "Top Secret"
- **1 gold watch** (or the watch prop found in the resource section of nazarene.org/vbs). This will be used for the closing skit.
- **Special Agent Tre** (Code Name: Trinity); dressed like a spy, with a hat and sunglasses
- **Agent-In-Training Buddy** (Code Name: Barnabas); dressed in street clothes but now wearing a hat like Tre
- **Agent Strange**; dressed as much like Tre as possible

Note: Use any additional props available to increase interest. Encourage the characters to move often and to use the whole platform/stage.

Dialogue:

Agent Tre: Hi kids! It's great to see you again! I have something super fun to show you in the special agent lockbox!

Buddy: *(Comes tiptoeing in, looking at invisible footprints on the ground with a magnifying glass. Intent on following the footprints, Buddy runs into Tre, bonks his head, and looks up surprised, not realizing he was following Tre's path.)*

Oh, Agent Tre! It's you! Oh, man, what IS today's passcode? Oh yeah! *(Stands at attention)* **Jesus' power transforms my life!** I wasn't sure this special agent magnifying glass would actually work...but it really does because I was able to follow YOUR tracks. YES!

Agent Tre: It's good to see you, Buddy! I have something to show you. *(Tre goes to the lockbox and starts to scan his thumbprint.)*

Agent Strange: *(Enters holding out an envelope to Tre)* Agent Tre? I have special orders for you from the Boss.

Buddy: Another special agent? Oh, this should be good! *(Buddy plops down on the chair for a good "show." During the next dialogue, Buddy exaggeratedly looks back and forth between each speaker as if watching a tennis match.)*

Agent Tre: *(Confused)* Orders from the Boss? But He always gives me my orders Himself.

Agent Strange: *(A bit hesitant)*…Uh…Yes, I know, but this time He wanted me to deliver them to you.

Agent Tre: *(Looking the envelope over)* Well…these LOOK like the orders I get from the Boss…*(Opens the envelope, pulls out a letter, and reads it to himself while moving his lips.)* But they don't sound at all like the Boss's orders. I need to call Him to verify.

Agent Strange: *(Looks scared)* NO! YOU CAN'T…I mean…you don't NEED to do that, Agent Trinity. After all, the Agent Handbook says in Isaiah 1:19 that "you will eat the good of the land **if you obey**." That means you should follow orders without question!

Agent Tre: Whoa! Now hang on just a minute! Jesus came to take away our sins, not our minds! I *always* follow the Boss's orders without question. What I'm questioning right now is whether these really *are* the Boss's orders! The Handbook also says in 1 Thessalonians 5:21 that I am to "test everything and hold fast to what is good." Before I do anything, I need to make sure these orders are the real deal, because counterfeiting the Boss' orders is exactly the kind of sneaky, lowdown, underhanded, dirty trick that Deceptor would try. So you just wait a minute while I check in with the Boss. *(Takes off his shoe to "make a call.")*

Agent Strange: *(Now very nervous)* I was told to deliver that envelope and that's exactly what I did. So I have done my job and I am OUT of here. *(Hurries offstage)*

Agent Tre: *(Into his shoe)* **Jesus' power transforms my life!** Boss, this is Agent Tre. A stranger just handed me an envelope and said he was delivering special orders from You. He *looked* like an agent, but I've never seen him before. No sir, he did not identify himself. Now that you mention it, he didn't give today's passcode either, and I should have asked for that right away. That's on me, sir, but that's why I'm calling. So You didn't send him? That's what I suspected, because those so-called "orders" didn't sound like anything You would ask me to do. Thank you, sir, I appreciate that! Goodbye to You, sir. *(Tre puts his shoe back on and rips up the envelope.)*

Buddy: Whoa, wait a minute! What just happened? *(Buddy stands up, interested.)*

Agent Tre: Well, Buddy, I don't know who that fellow was, but he was NOT a special agent and those were NOT orders from the Boss! I messed up by not asking him for today's passcode. That's why we need to be self-controlled and alert, because you never know when Deceptor's going to try to pull a fast one on you.

Buddy: But how did you KNOW he wasn't an agent and those weren't orders from the Boss? He sure looked like an agent. And he even quoted the Agent Handbook!

Agent Tre: That's true, Buddy, but always remember that Deceptor is a master of disguises. And he quoted from the Handbook when he tried to tempt the Boss Himself! If all it took to be a special agent was to dress like one and memorize a few lines in the Handbook, we'd all be in trouble. But it's not just what's on the outside that counts, it's what's on the inside!

Buddy: But how can we keep from being fooled?

Agent Tre: Well, for starters, there's the daily passcode. But the main thing is spending time with the Boss. The more time I spend with Him, the easier it is to tell the difference between good and evil and right and wrong. Always remember that people have quoted bits and pieces of the Agent Handbook for years to justify whatever they want to do. That's why it's important to know the WHOLE Handbook and not just a few favorite parts.

Buddy: That ability to tell the difference between good and evil and right and wrong—is that some kind of super power that only a few special agents have?

Agent Tre: Oh, no Buddy! The Boss gives that ability to all of His agents. That's why it's called *Operation Transformation!*

Remember when Agent Paul was called Saul and he was arresting all the Christians? It was only after he encountered Jesus that he realized what he was doing was wrong.

Buddy: I remember! Saul was told to go to a certain house on Straight Street, and then this guy named Ananias came and placed his hands on him, told him what God said, and suddenly he could see again.

Agent Tre: Wow, Buddy! You really *were* listening during yesterday's lesson! That's very impressive! When Saul met Jesus, everything changed, because that's what Jesus does! What's today's passcode?

Buddy: **Jesus' power transforms my life!**

Agent Tre: Exactly!

Buddy: What happened next? To Saul…or Paul…or whatever his name was! *(Buddy sits down, interested)*

Agent Tre: Well, he stayed with the people Jesus sent him to live with, because he knew he had a lot to learn. He knew how to *persecute* Christians, but he didn't know how to *be* one! But before long he was telling people what Jesus had done for him and openly declaring that Jesus is the Son of God! That really made his old friends mad because they still hated Jesus and they really hated anyone who said Jesus was God's Son. So they made plans to kill Saul. But the Boss warned him about their plans.

Buddy: How did he get away?

Agent Tre: His new Christian friends waited until it got dark, then they lowered him over the city wall in a big basket. That's how he escaped!

Buddy: Yes! *(Fist pumps)* Man, that was close! But I guess he had to lay low after that so he couldn't preach anymore or tell people about Jesus.

Agent Tre: No way! Saul the persecutor had become Paul the special agent, and he was on a mission from God! Once he discovered the truth about Jesus, that truth had set him free! So he wanted everyone else to know it too, so they could be transformed like him!

Buddy: He did a total 180! He went from hating Jesus and His followers to *becoming* a Jesus-follower! Talk about a radical transformation. People must have thought he was crazy.

Agent Tre: I know. It doesn't really make sense until you actually *know Jesus* yourself and then it makes perfect sense…but only afterwards. Look at this! *("Scans" thumb print on the lockbox and takes out the butterfly picture.)*

Buddy: OK…It's a butterfly! What does that have to do with today's lesson?

Agent Tre: You'll find out in the Mission Brief! Hang on! *(Takes off his shoe and answers the "phone")* **Jesus' power transforms my life!** Yes, sir! I'll leave right away.

Buddy: Another mission?

Agent Tre: Yes indeed! Want to come?

Buddy: Absolutely!!! *(Buddy jumps up and runs after Tre)* See you later, kids!

Director: I wonder what their mission is today! I hope they are back in time for our closing! In the meantime, we had better get to our Transformation Stations; we have a lot to learn today.

Closing:

If time allows, sing 1-2 songs focused on sanctifying power, Jesus our Lord, surrender, or trust.

End with Day 2 Song, "John 10:27, My sheep listen to my voice," with hand motions.

Kids are dismissed by groups and given any instructions they need to get to their Transformation Station.

Play theme song as children exit.

DAY TWO

Transformation Station

MISSION BRIEF: CATERPILLAR SOUP

Learn about the transformation that takes place in a caterpillar as it becomes a butterfly and consider the transformation we experience as we become more and more like Jesus.

Preparation:
- If possible, the leader should wear a **white lab coat**.
- Prepare a **large manila envelope** with "MISSON BRIEF #2" written in large letters on the outside. Place a copy of the **script** inside.
- Have the **flower** from yesterday close by to review as a well as a **picture** of how it looked yesterday.
- Gather copies of the **Mission Brief Day 2 sheet** for every child (found in the resource section of nazarene.org/vbs).
- If possible, be ready to show the **video**.
- Have a current **NIV Bible** with your supplies.

Directions:
View the links below of videos and pictures of the life cycle of the butterfly. Choose which if any you want to show the children. Print the Mission Brief Day 2 sheet for each child if possible. Consider how you want to teach metamorphosis.

Options:
- youtube.com/watch?v=WcokL7PRrnY
- youtube.com/watch?v=ocWgSgMGxOc
- youtube.com/watch?v=V5RSpMQQOpw
- Video for older kids or just to equip you as a teacher: youtube.com/watch?v=AZk6nZGH9Xo
- Pictures: thebutterflysite.com/life-cycle.shtml

Review:

Day 1: **Jesus' love transforms my identity.**
How is our white flower today?

(Draw out the conclusion that the longer you spend "soaking" in the Word of God and being with God's people, the more you begin looking like a child of God. Compare the pictures of the flower placed in the red water yesterday to the flower prepped a week ago. There should be increased transformation over time.)

Mission Brief Summary:

(Feel free to make this your own!)

1. Retell the Saul meets the disciples story in **Acts 9:20-30.** (Jesus' power transformed Saul's life.)
2. Review yesterday. Retell Saul's experience in Damascus, his escape, and his introduction to the disciples in Jerusalem. God's power continued to transform Saul as he spent time with the disciples in Damascus and in Jerusalem. Saul trusted God and followed Him through situations Saul never dreamed he would face. God continued to strengthen Saul's faith and transform him into Christlikeness.
3. Explain the transformation of the caterpillar into a butterfly. This is an example of God's transforming power at work. God's power can also transform us.
4. Invite the children into a transformational relationship with Jesus.

Mission Brief Leader Suggested Script:

(Feel free to adapt to your context.)

Today we will learn even more about transformation. Does anyone remember what Agent Tre pulled out of the lockbox today? *(Pause for answers)*
Right!

Why do you think he told us to study the butterfly today? I'm sure it has something to do with today's special agent passcode: **Jesus' power transforms my life!** A butterfly is an awesome example of one thing being totally transformed into something else. Who knows what this butterfly was before it became a butterfly? *(Pause for answers)*
Right! A caterpillar!

(Go over the life cycle of the butterfly videos or pictures.)

What most people do not realize is that when a caterpillar is in the cocoon in the pupa stage, it does not just grow legs and wings and "poof," become a butterfly. It dissolves into a sort of caterpillar "soup." The caterpillar is made of proteins that are completely disassembled. Miraculously, a butterfly is REMADE from the bits of what used to be something that looked very different. It is like God recycles the caterpillar and reshapes it. God transforms it into a beautiful butterfly.

Perhaps the most amazing thing is that there is scientific evidence that the butterfly has memories of being a caterpillar! So it doesn't totally forget where it came from, even after it has been transformed.

The metamorphosis of the caterpillar helps us to understand what happens when God transforms us through a new relationship with Jesus. When God comes into our lives, He does not just add a few good things to who we already are. He remakes us and gives us an entirely new identity with a new purpose and new priorities. We begin to love the things God loves and want the things that God wants.

Remember our passcode today: **Jesus' power transforms my life!**

Can anyone remember the transformation of Saul?

The Bible says that when Saul could not see, his friends took him into Damascus where he waited for three days without eating or drinking. Saul did just as Jesus had said. He waited until he was told what to do next. Then God sent Ananias, who prayed for Saul and God restored Saul's sight. The first thing Saul did after he could see again was to be baptized. He wanted to show the world that he was now a follower of Jesus. Then it says that Saul spent several days with the disciples in Damascus.

This time of waiting for Ananias to come when Saul was blind and then the time Saul spent with his new brothers in Christ reminds me of the time a caterpillar spends in his cocoon! It is a time of un-making and re-making. Saul was learning a new way of seeing God and listening to Him. Saul was learning God's ways and God's priorities.

Look what the Bible says in the next two verses! "At once he began to preach in the synagogues that Jesus is the Son of God. All those who heard him were astonished and asked, 'Isn't he the man who raised havoc in Jerusalem among those who call on this name? And hasn't he come here to take them as prisoners to the chief priests?'" (Acts 9:20-21). People were amazed and were witnesses to the fact that the time Saul spent in Jesus' presence had so powerfully transformed him that he was living a completely transformed life. His priorities were completely opposite from where they had been. In fact, Acts 9:22 says, "Saul grew more and more powerful and baffled the Jews living in Damascus by proving that Jesus is the Messiah!"

Saul's transformation was so radical that the Jews planned to kill him. Saul's friends helped him escape to Jerusalem. The Christians in Jerusalem did not accept Saul right away. They knew Saul's reputation and were not sure if he could be trusted, but Barnabas spoke up for Saul and the disciples decided to give him a chance. They must have seen how God had transformed Saul's heart and life. Saul went from persecuting Christians to becoming a Christian, from *knowing about* Jesus to *knowing* Jesus as Lord and Savior.

(If appropriate and time allows, leaders should share their transformation story. What was your life like before you came to know Jesus? How are you different now? Share an invitation for children to begin this life of transformation. See Leading a Child to Christ in the resource section of nazarene.org/vbs.)

Seeing a butterfly or a caterpillar can remind us of God's transforming power at work in the world. Let's say today's code together before you head to your next transformation station, **"Jesus' power transforms my life!"**

DAY TWO

Transformation Station

**EVIDENCE VAULT:
JOHN 10:27**

Play the theme song or memory verse song as children enter the room. Open your time with the top secret hand signal.

Supplies:

- Recording of the day's **memory verse song**
- **Memory verse chart**
- Optional **prizes or mission money**
- **Supplies for memory verse game** from the resource section of nazarene.org/vbs

Evidence Vault Leader Suggested Script:

Who remembers today's secret passcode? *(Pause for answers)*
Jesus' power transforms my life!

Our verse today helps us better understand the passcode.

John 10:27
"My sheep listen to my voice; I know them, and they follow me."

(If time allows and they are catching on quickly, you can add John 10:28a: "I give them eternal life, and they shall never perish.")

These are Jesus' words! Jesus talked in parables or stories to help people understand what He was saying. In those days, where Jesus lived, shepherds were common. Everyone in Jesus' audience understood what He meant when He said, "My sheep listen to my voice; I know them and they follow me."

You see, sheep become very close to their shepherds. Shepherds carefully watch over their sheep and protect them. When their sheep get hurt, shepherds use special oil to help heal them. When sheep get lost, shepherds go looking for them. Shepherds lead sheep carefully because they need special care and could get hurt easily. Sheep recognize the voice of their shepherd. When it is time to gather the flock at night, the shepherd calls to them and they come to him. When two shepherds have been in the field together, they don't have a to be concerned about mixing up their sheep. Sheep will follow the voice of their shepherd. A good shepherd loves his sheep, and his sheep feel safe and will follow him.

Jesus wasn't just talking about *animals* when He shared our memory verse with the people of the Bible. Jesus was talking about the *people* that follow Him. He was using a word picture. He was saying, "I'm a shepherd to my people. I take care of the people that follow me. These people listen to my voice. I know each of them myself and my people follow me!"

He also said, "They will never follow a stranger; in fact, they will run away from him because they do not recognize a stranger's voice."

How do you think the sheep know the shepherd's voice? *(Pause for answers)*
They spend time with him.

How do you think we can know Jesus' voice so we can follow Him? How can you spend time with Jesus if you can't see Him?
- He left us the Bible so we could get to know Him.
- We can learn how to follow Him by obeying what the Bible says.
- We can pray and talk with Him.
- When we pray, we can listen for Him to speak.
- Jesus gives us His Spirit to help us know good from bad and to help us do what pleases Him.
- We can memorize His words (the Bible) so we can tell when we are hearing His voice. As His people, we obey His voice and follow Him only.
- We can practice a heart of thankfulness, which teaches us to see Him in everything.

Saul listened to Jesus and followed Him, and God's power totally transformed Saul's life.

Closing:

Outline the plan your church has made to reward children that memorize Scripture this week. A downloadable memory verse chart is provided for you to write the children's names and keep track of who has memorized which verses. Allow them time each day to repeat them to you.

Go over the memory verse several times.

If they are ready, have children come to you individually to say their verse. Mark it on the memory verse chart. If you are giving prizes or secret mission money for saying today's portion of the verse, hand them out now.

If time allows, play a memory verse game from the memory verse games resource.

DAY TWO

Transformation Station

CRAFT LAB: BUTTERFLY FOOTPRINTS

Play the theme song and the memory verse song as children arrive. Ask the children to repeat the memory verse or the passcode for the day.

Directions:

Create a butterfly while talking about God's transforming power. View the link for detailed instructions and a list of supplies.

- mommypotamus.com/how-to-make-butterfly-footprint-art

Tip: When making hand and footprint art, use washable paint or stamp pads and have plenty of baby wipes close by to immediately clean paint from children's hands and feet.

Allow plenty of time and invite extra helpers to join in the fun. Add the Bible verse for the day or the phrase **"Jesus' power transforms my life"** to the bottom of the child's artwork to remind them of our theme.

Craft Lab Leader Suggested Script:

Just like God transforms a caterpillar into a beautiful butterfly, Jesus' power transformed Saul's life. His power transforms our lives, too, especially when we follow Jesus like Saul!

Most of us do not see a blinding light and I have never seen a person transformed in a cocoon! God transformed Saul's life in an amazing way. It all started on the road to Damascus, but it didn't stop there. God continued His transforming work in Saul as Saul listened to and followed God.

Do you remember our memory verse? **"My sheep listen to my voice; I know them and they follow me" (John 10:27).** When we respond to God, His transforming power helps us to hear Him and follow Him while He continues to work in us as we grow more and more like Jesus.

DAY TWO

Transformation Station

RECHARGE STATION: SHEEP SNACKS

Play the theme song and the memory verse song as children arrive. Ask the children to repeat the memory verse or passcode for the day.

Directions:

Follow the supplies and directions according to your choice from the list below.
- dancingthroughtherain.com/no-bake-sheep-grahams
- kraftrecipes.com/recipe/211788/fluffy-marshmallow-sheep

Recharge Station Leader Suggested Script:

In the Bible, Jesus often uses sheep to explain how people behave. Even today if you go to Israel, you will see shepherds taking their sheep out to graze on hillsides. The most amazing sight is when two shepherds have been talking and their sheep have gotten all mixed up together as they graze on the hillside. When the two shepherds decide it is time to part ways, one shepherd walks one direction while calling their sheep and the other shepherd walks another way and calls to their sheep. What looks like a pile of sheep all of the sudden starts sorting this way and that way. Each sheep knows his shepherd's voice and follows! Those sheep would never follow another shepherd's voice!

Does that remind you of the memory verse we learned earlier today?

"My sheep listen to my voice; I know them and they follow me" (John 10:27).

Jesus also said this about His sheep, "…they will never follow a stranger; in fact, they will run away from him because they do not recognize a stranger's voice" (John 10:5).

Remember when Agent Tre was given phony instructions from the fake agent? He did NOT listen to them because they did not sound right. He double-checked with the Boss…that's what we do when we belong to Jesus. When we are unsure about what is right, we talk to God about it. We listen for His answer.

What does God's voice sound like? *(Share how you have heard God speak before.)* Sometimes God's voice sounds like a small voice inside us telling us right from wrong. Some people call this our conscience. Sometimes our parents, teachers, or even our Christian friends can share what God has shown them to be true in their own lives.

How can we know if it is God's voice or the enemy's voice or our own? Great question!

1. God will never ask us to do anything that the Bible says we should not do. This is why it is so important for us to know God's Word and to memorize it!
2. God's Holy Spirit lives inside every believer and helps us know what is right and what is wrong. When you accept Jesus as your Savior and Lord, He sends the Holy Spirit to be your helper and friend.
3. The Bible says if we are not sure if something is God's will, we can talk to other Christians.

Is there anyone here who has any questions about what it is like to follow Jesus? *(Let children ask their questions and pray for wisdom. If you are unsure how to answer, let the child know it is a wonderful question, write it down, and let them know you will find out and get back to them. And follow-up!)*

DAY TWO

Transformation Station

AGENT TRAINING FIELD: FOLLOW ME

Equipment:
- Blindfold
- A "prize" (a ball or toy)

Objective:
Find the "prize" by following the leader's voice.

How to Play the Game:
Begin by having all children stand in the circle. The leader shows the "prize" to all the children. One child volunteer is blindfolded and placed in the center of the circle.

The leader gives the instructions.

"You are going to follow my voice. I want you to listen super closely, because if you follow my voice, I will lead you to the prize. Your job is to listen and follow my voice. As soon as you get the prize, you may take the blindfold off. It will be difficult for you, because ALL of the people in the circle are going to try to tell you things. They are going to be yelling instructions at you that may or may not be correct. But I will lead you to the prize, so always listen for my voice."

Count down to begin and when you say "go," everyone starts yelling instructions to the person to turn right, turn left, back up, straight ahead, two steps, etc. Only the leader's voice is telling the right instructions.

Memory Verse Application:

(After you have played several times) Was it easy or hard to get the prize? *(Pause for answers)*

How did you find the prize? *(Pause for answers)*
Had to stop, concentrate, listen carefully for the leader. The more they listened, the more they were able to drown out other voices and just hear the voice of the leader.

This is like our walk with God. Sometimes other things or people can distract us from God and the choices He wants us to make. We have to stop, concentrate, ask God for help, and listen for God's voice. It is important that we recognize God's voice among all the others and obey Him. Listening to His instructions will help us know right from wrong.

Where can we go to understand what God would have us do? *(Pause for answers)*
Bible, church, mom and dad.

That is why it is always good to spend time reading God's Word.

DAY TWO

Transformation Station

INFILTRATION SERVICE PROJECT

Do something that will transform someone's day.

Remember:

The importance of this activity is to teach the children the value of reaching out to others, so no matter the activity you choose, point to the fact that this gift represents the transformation that takes place when we give our lives to Jesus.

You can write a note to be delivered with each gift that the children sign. A note might say something like, "At VBS this week, we are learning that God's power transforms our lives when we live for Him. May God bless you with the power of His transforming love!"

Ideas:

- Make cards for those in the church who are elderly or unable to leave their homes.
- Send cards or Scripture to encourage those in the church who serve in the military and on the mission field.
- Draw pictures or make cards for firefighters or police officers and encourage families to deliver them to the station together.
- Make cards for those who serve others, like postal workers or trash collectors.
- Draw pictures for someone in the church who is sick. Include Scripture to encourage them.
- Work on the church property to transform a small area into something beautiful (pull weeds, plant flowers, pick up the nursery toys and organize them for the younger children, etc.).

DAY TWO

Closing Skit

Play theme song and memory verse song as children return.

Ask volunteers to share the passcode, memory verse, favorite activity, or something they learned. Or have trivia questions prepared to ask early arrivers.

Begin with the top secret hand signal.

Dialogue:

Buddy: Whew! That was the longest mission in the history of FOREVER! Seriously, Agent Tre, why couldn't you just pick out any old watch? That was just WAY too long to wait for you!

Agent Tre: *(Laughs)* You're funny, Buddy. Some missions take a long time. We don't go on missions because they're fun—even though they sometimes are. We go on missions to help others, because that's what agents do!

Buddy: *(Interrupts, almost acts bored)* Yeah, yeah, yeah, I know…But we didn't actually help anyone at the mall, did we? Was that really a mission, buying a watch?

Agent Tre: Of course it was a mission! Anything the Boss tells me to do is a mission. It wasn't just ANY mall and it wasn't just any watch.

Buddy: *(Plops down, exhausted, on the floor or chair and quotes, sarcastically)* Oh, I know because we looked for it for three straight hours! "A gold watch with special engraving."

Agent Tre: *(Pulls out the pocket watch)* Well, that's where your magnifying glass came in handy, Buddy! I knew it was the right one because it's engraved with the Boss's seal. *(Tre shows the watch to Buddy. Buddy gets out his magnifying glass.)* See that triangle? It represents God the Father, God the Son, and God the Holy Spirit—3 in 1.

Buddy: Oh, I see it! But why did the Boss send you to buy that watch?

Agent Tre: I don't know. My job is to trust Him and obey. Sometimes we never know the reason behind a mission. Sometimes He's protecting us. Like in our Bible story today. He told the disciples in Damascus to get Saul out of the city secretly. Sometimes we find out later how our mission helped someone else. And sometimes we never know why—but the Boss always has a reason.

Buddy: Ok…well then, why did you have to buy the watch with your own money? Why didn't the Boss give you the money to buy it?

Agent Tre: Well, actually, when I became an agent, I realized that everything I have comes from Him anyway and He supplies all of my needs through His glorious riches in Christ Jesus…so He actually did give me the money to buy it.

Buddy: Is it scary? Trusting Him like that?

Agent Tre: That's a great question, Buddy. The truth is it can be scary to trust completely, at least at first. But He has never broken a promise, and I know He really will take care of me because He always has. Now I don't even think about it. I just trust Him and follow what I know He tells me to do. The more I trust Him and obey, the more God shows how He is at work in my life. As I have followed Him, He has transformed what I want into more and more what He wants for me. Because He wants what is the very best for me, it is easier and easier to trust and follow Him.

Buddy: *(All of the sudden very interested)* Ooh! So I can have whatever I want just by asking Him?!

Agent Tre: *(Laughs)* I didn't say that. He always supplies my NEEDS, not all my WANTS. Just like He always answers prayer. Sometimes the answer is "yes" and at other times the answer is "no." And sometimes the answer is "wait." I can always trust that God is at work and wants the best for me.

Buddy: *(Jumps up, like a lightbulb just went off in his head)* Oh, I get it! I get it! When I realize how much God loves me and cares about me, I know I can trust Him no matter what. And when I realize I can trust Him completely, then I can follow wherever He leads me because that will always be the best choice for me. So when I choose to trust and follow Him, that's when God is at work transforming me. Have I got that right, Tre?

Agent Tre: *(Smiling huge, grabbing Buddy for a big bear hug)* I couldn't have said it better myself! Come on, Buddy! Let's get something to eat. I'm buying! See you tomorrow, kids!

Director: See you tomorrow, Tre and Buddy! What an amazing God! We have learned a lot about God's transforming power today. It is incredible to realize that God cares so much about the details of our lives that He actually will guide us as we trust and follow Him. Just like with Saul, God's power can transform our life, too. When we obey and follow God, we get a chance to see Him at work. God does some amazing things through His people and when we see God working, it changes us. Imagine if you were Saul and knew God was using His disciples to save your life by lowering you in a basket to get you secretly out of the city. Wow! That took trust! And just think how much more you would trust God once you lived through it and shared what God had done with others. God loves us so much that we can always trust that He wants what is best for us.

God has given us another great day at *Operation Transformation!* While you were in your Transformation Stations, we counted the offering. Do you want to know who gave the most today, the girls or the boys?

The girls gave $_____ and the boys gave $_____! So who gave the most? *(Pause for answers)* Right! But working together, you gave _____ to the real winners: children all around the world who will hear about *Operation Transformation* because of your unselfish generosity. Way to go!

Everyone please stand for our closing prayer: Thank You, God, for Your transforming power and love for each one of us and for the generosity of these children. We pray that you will help other children know You and Your Son, Jesus! Amen.

Everyone take off your nametags and give them to your group leader. You can pick them up when you come back tomorrow. OK? And everybody remember to bring a friend, so they can hear about *Operation Transformation* too!

Closing:
Give any other announcements or direction for dismissal. Play theme song as children leave.

OPERATION TRANSFORMATION

DAY THREE

DAY THREE

Table of Contents

Week at a Glance 4

Leadership Meeting 6

Opening & Welcome 8

Opening Skit 10

Transformation Stations 14
    Mission Brief 14
    Evidence Vault 18
    Craft Lab 20
    Recharge Station 22
    Agent Training Field 24
    Infiltration Service Project 26

Closing Skit **27**

DAY THREE

Leadership Meeting

- Greeting and appreciation
- Our goal is to *help kids experience life-transforming encounters with Jesus Christ.*
- Review training meeting highlights (bathroom policy, safety policy, discipline, what to do in case of illness or emergency, releasing children at day's end, etc.). Since the details were provided at a prior training, offer these on a single printed page as a reminder.
- Remind leaders of the special offering project.

Day 3 Overview:

Today's Passcode:	Today's Theology Focus:	Today's Bible Story:
Jesus' presence transforms my choices	**Sustaining** Use every opportunity to weave this into your time with the kids.	**Acts 16:16-34** (read aloud)

Review Today's Memory Verse:

Psalm 25:9
"He guides the humble in what is right and teaches them his way."

Review Top Secret Hand Signal:

Tap-tap, clap-clap, snap-snap, SHHHHHH!

Pat palms on top of legs two times, clap hands two times, snap fingers two times, and place finger to lips while shushing. NOTE: some people have difficulty snapping their fingers; encourage them to close all four fingers onto their palms.

- Review today's songs. Motions to Psalm 25:9 are included on the media section of nazarene.org/vbs.
- Review today's schedule.
- Questions, comments, or concerns?
- Close with prayer at least 15 minutes before start time.

OUR PRAYER FOR YOU:

Father God, we worship You for Who You are.

There is no one like You, Who loves, seeks, and saves the lost.

All of our preparation has brought us to this moment.

Now, Father, bring the children You know need to be here today.

Cut out all distractions so the Good News will go forth without hindrance.

Give us ears to hear Your Spirit and the right words to communicate Your love to the children.

Help us remember what we have prepared to present to the children today.

Give us the energy and enthusiasm to make Your Word

as exciting, engaging, and powerful as it truly is.

We pray the children will fall in love with You and with Your Word.

Draw them by Your grace into a right relationship with you.

Grant us strength to carry out Your work here today.

Protect these kids and these workers.

Take care of our families at home while we seek to expand your Kingdom here.

May Your Kingdom come and Your will be done here today.

We will be careful to give You all the glory.

In Jesus' name and for the sake of His Kingdom,

Amen.

DAY THREE

Opening & Welcome

Be prepared to transition quickly from music to dialogue to music to skit to keep attention focused.

Sing Theme Song and Day 1 and 2 Songs with Hand Motions

Starting with music engages everyone's attention and participation.

Welcome

The following is a suggested script:

Director: Welcome to Day Three of *Operation Transformation!* I am Special Agent _____ and it's so great to see all of you today! I have been looking forward to seeing you and going on our mission today. We are going to have a great day! Did you remember our Bible verse for the week? *(Say the verse you just sang.)*

We have already learned two other verses. Who knows John 1:12? *(Pause for answers)*

Does anyone remember our passcode for Day 1? It has something to do with becoming children of God…*(Pause for answers)*
That is right! "Jesus' love transforms my identity!"

Yesterday we learned about hearing God's voice and that He transforms us when we follow Him. Who can remember our verse for yesterday, John 10:27? *(Pause for answers)*

Does anyone remember the passcode from yesterday? *(Pause for answers)*
That's right! "Jesus' power transforms my life!" You have really been paying attention!

Today is a super exciting Bible story about the adventure of Saul as he continues to follow Jesus! I can't wait for you to hear about it because when you do, you will really understand the passcode for today. Despite our circumstances, Jesus' presence can transform our choices! In fact, that is today's passcode—say it with me, **"Jesus' presence transforms my choices!"** Let's hear the boys!…Let's hear the girls!…Now all together! **"Jesus' presence transforms my choices!"**

We also have a new verse today and it is good news! We don't have to figure out the right choices on our own. **Psalm 25:9** says, **"He guides the humble in what is right and teaches them his way."** That was true for Saul and I'm so glad it is true for us today.

Offering

Director: Who can share what our offering is for this week? *(Share about your mission project for those who may be new. You can find information about the Kids Reaching Kids Offering at nazarene.org/sdmi.)* That's right. So far you have given $_____ towards our project. We are going to sing our new verse for the day and learn the motions while you bring your offering. Don't worry if you don't have anything to give today, follow your leader anyway. Now that you know, you can bring it tomorrow! We'll all meet back here before you go home and that's when we'll see if the GIRLS or BOYS won!

(Play today's memory verse song and receive the offering. Use this time to make any other special announcements. When everyone has returned to their seats, lead them in the top secret hand signal to get their attention.)

Great job everyone! You just heard today's memory verse song. We'll be singing it all day—but of course we need to learn it first! So let's sing it one more time before we meet Agent Tre and Buddy to find out about today's mission.

Sing Theme Song with Hand Motions

Sing Day 3 Song with Hand Motions

DAY THREE

Opening Skit

Props & Characters:

- **Special agent lockbox**, marked "Top Secret"
- **1-2 Mission Brief Day 3 sheets** found in the resource section of nazarene.org/vbs. (These are placed in the lockbox with an NIV Bible and a flashlight.)
- **NIV Bible** (Place in the lockbox.)
- **Flashlight** (Place in the lockbox.)
- **1-2 chairs**
- **Special Agent Tre** (Code Name: Trinity); dressed like a spy, with a hat and sunglasses
- **Agent-In-Training Buddy** (Code Name: Barnabas); dressed like a spy, with a hat *but not sunglasses* (see Day Four Skits)
- **Agent Strange**; dressed as much like Tre as possible

Note: Use any additional props available to increase interest. Encourage the characters to move often and to use the whole platform/stage.

Dialogue:

Agent Strange: *("Sneaking around")* I really thought I had him yesterday. That Trinity makes me so MAD! He's doing MY job. Yesterday I thought I could get him distracted by giving him that fake assignment…everything was just right. The envelope looked exactly like the ones my dad used to get. I thought I had Tre fooled. Why did he have to mess everything up by calling the Boss? I underestimated how hard it will be to get him out of my way. I'll just have to try harder today!

If I can trap him while he's out on a mission and hide him away, they'll have no choice but to make me a REAL agent because then they'll need me! I just need to figure out a plan…Yes! I know just what to do! *(Rubbing his hands together, Strange leaves stage with a triumphant "evil laugh")*

(Buddy and Agent Tre enter stage opposite Strange)

Buddy: Hey Tre! Did the Boss ever tell you what to do with that watch He had you purchase yesterday?

Agent Tre: *(Distracted, reading something)*

Buddy: Tre? Agent Trinity?

Agent Tre: Oh, sorry Buddy…Uh, no. The Boss didn't tell me what to do with the watch. Sometimes we don't get to see the big picture. I just do what He asks me to do and await further instructions.

Buddy: You seem distracted today. What's going on?

Agent Tre: I'm reading something incredible in the Agent Handbook *(Goes back to reading)*.

Buddy: O…K…would you…care to share?

Agent Tre: Oh! Sure, Buddy. It's the official account of Paul's wrongful imprisonment.

Buddy: Wrongful imprisonment? What's that?

Agent Tre: It's when someone is falsely accused and thrown in jail when they didn't do anything wrong. It's all right here in Acts 16:16-40. It happened after Paul had received his new identity and God's power had transformed him. He was even following God. This is one of the stories that shows how God Himself was with Paul. He was Paul's help and friend when Paul was in trouble.

Buddy: God was Paul's help and friend. I like that…but what does that have to do with prison?

Agent Tre: Paul was following God, doing good, and helping people. He went to a city called Philippi with his friend Silas. The city leaders didn't worship God. They wanted Paul and Silas to stop doing miracles and getting people all excited about Jesus. So they had them beaten and jailed in the deepest, darkest part of the prison.

Buddy: Just for helping people and telling them about Jesus? That's not fair!

Agent Tre: You're right; it's not! But the enemy doesn't fight fair. When people hear about the good news of Jesus and accept His love, their lives are transformed. Those who are slaves to sin are set free. But slave owners never want their slaves set free! So Paul and Silas found themselves beaten up and jailed. But they knew they had been doing God's will. They began thinking about God's great love and started thanking Him for sending Jesus. That's when they were filled with joy despite their suffering and started singing praise songs to God!

Buddy: WHAT? They had just been beaten and jailed for obeying God! Why would they praise God when He allowed them to get beat up just for doing what He told them to do?

Agent Tre: Bad things happen to ALL people, Buddy. But when bad things happen to US, we have the advantage of knowing God is right there with us. He never leaves us. His power is at work in us helping us to do what He has asked us to do.

Buddy: I never thought of it like that before. I guess good and bad things happen to everyone. But that's still nothing to celebrate and sing about.

Agent Tre: They weren't singing because bad things happened to them. They were singing because God was right there with them. And it wasn't long before God showed His power to everyone in that jail. There was a massive earthquake, everyone's chains fell off, and all the cell doors flew open!

Buddy: Woah! I bet they got out of there as fast as they could.

Agent Tre: That's exactly what the head jailer thought. And even though it wasn't his fault, he thought his life was over because he knew the city leaders would blame him for the prisoners' escape! But Paul yelled, "Hey! It's OK! We're still here!" That's when the jailer realized there was something very different about Paul and Silas! He realized he needed help from *their* God, so he asked them, "Sirs, what must I do to be saved?" and they replied, "Believe in the Lord Jesus, and you will be saved…"

Buddy: That's it? "Believe in the Lord Jesus, and you will be saved!" It's really that simple?

Agent Tre: Absolutely!

Buddy: Hmmm…*(Seems distracted but shakes himself out of it)* What happened next?

Agent Tre: The jailer took Paul and Silas into his home, cleaned and bandaged their wounds, and fed them a meal. Paul and Silas told him about Jesus, and that night the jailer and his entire family were saved!

Buddy: Wow! And none of that would have happened if they hadn't been thrown in jail!

Agent Tre: None of that would have happened if they hadn't been in jail *and* singing praises to God! That's a great lesson to remember, Buddy. Sometimes God sends us into difficult places because that's where the lost people are. God wants them to be saved and He works through us to make that happen—*especially* in tough situations. That's why it's SO important to complete the mission without griping or complaining, especially when we're treated unfairly because that really surprises people. It makes them wonder what's going on with us and that curiosity gives us a chance to tell them about Jesus!

Buddy: I get it! Hey, speaking of curiosity…I wonder what's in the special agent lockbox today? Do you think maybe I can open it today? After all, I have been on secret missions with you and I've learned to dress like you, so I'm a whole lot more like you than I used to be. So my thumbprint ought to work today! *(Buddy tries it. It doesn't work.)* Why isn't it working? I'm doing everything you're doing!

Agent Tre: Buddy, you're talking about things on the outside: how you dress, how you act, what you do. Remember Agent Strange? He looks and acts the part too, but *he is definitely not a special agent!* God isn't fooled by appearances or acting. God looks on the inside; He sees what's in our hearts! There's a huge difference between *knowing about* Jesus and *knowing* Jesus as your friend and savior. Until you receive Him into your heart as your Lord and Savior, you're not a special agent and your thumbprint won't work. But I'm confident you will be one day, if you just don't give up, Buddy. *(Pats Buddy on the shoulder in a kind and caring gesture.)*

(Scans thumbprint, opens lockbox.) Hey, look at this! *(Gives the paper to Buddy and holds up a flashlight.)*

Buddy: I can't read that. What is it? Please bring that flashlight over. Looks like a bunch of weird lines and boxes.

Agent Tre: It's a secret coded message and the flashlight is not helping. Since neither one of us can read it, it must be a message for these new recruits. *(Points to the children)* Their mission brief leader will have to help them figure out what it says and why they might need a flashlight.

Buddy: Tre, is that your shoe ringing?

Agent Tre: It sure is, Buddy! Do you realize what just happened? You can hear my shoe phone! That means you're learning to listen! *(Speaking into his shoe)* Yes sir! Today's passcode is **Jesus' presence transforms my choices.** Yes sir, this is Agent Trinity. *(Pause)* Thank You, sir. I appreciate the reminder. *("Turns off" phone and returns it to his foot)*

Buddy: What's the mission?

Agent Tre: The Boss wanted to remind me that, "He guides the humble in what is right and teaches them His way."

Buddy: O…K…is that some sort of secret code too? Because that is a very strange mission!

Agent Tre: It's not a mission, Buddy, and it's not a secret code. The Boss is sending me a reminder that I'll need to remember for our next mission. He knows I've got a lot going on. Man…I think I'm gonna' need your help remembering this, Buddy.

Buddy: Sure! Maybe if we say it together…*(Walk off stage together, repeating the reminder.)* He guides the humble in what is right and teaches them His way…He guides the humble…

Director: I wonder if they're going to be all right. I thought I saw Agent Strange snooping around earlier. Did any of you see him? I thought so! I hope Buddy and Tre are going to be OK. I'll be sure to send the flashlight and the secret coded message to your mission brief station so you can figure out how to decode it to help Buddy and Tre!

Closing:

If time allows, sing 1-2 songs focused on God's sustaining presence, Jesus our friend, guide, and strength.

End with Day 3 Song, *"Psalm 25:9, He guides the humble,"* with hand motions.

Kids are dismissed by groups and given any instructions they need to get to their Transformation Station.

Play theme song as children exit.

DAY THREE

Transformation Station

**MISSION BRIEF:
DECODE GOD'S PERSPECTIVE**

Preparation:
- If possible, the leader should wear a **white lab coat**.
- Prepare a **large manila envelope** with "MISSION BRIEF #3" written in large letters on the outside. Place a copy of the **script** inside.
- Place a copy of the **Mission Brief Day 3 sheet** inside (found in the resource section of nazarene.org/vbs). Be sure you have practiced folding it correctly to reveal the messages.
- Have a **current NIV Bible** with your supplies.
- Have the **flashlight** from the opening.

Directions:
Play the song for today's verse as children arrive and leave. Look at the pictures provided and practice folding the paper prior to the lesson so that you are sure you know how to show the messages.

Review:

Day 1: Jesus' love transforms my identity.
How is our white flower today?

(Draw out the conclusion that the longer you spend "soaking" in the Word of God and being with God's people, the more you begin looking like a child of God.)

Day 2: Jesus' power transforms my life.
Who remembers what we learned in our mission brief yesterday?

(Butterflies transform completely and are totally re-made, just like we are when Jesus comes to live inside us!)

Mission Brief Summary:

(Feel free to make this your own!)

1. Retell the Paul in prison story in **Acts 16:16-34.** (Jesus' presence transformed Paul's choices.)
2. Explain that Paul had a relationship with Jesus that sustained him through hard times. Paul kept doing what was good and right, even when his life got hard (worshipping and praising God even when he was in prison). A relationship with Jesus transformed Paul into a light that pointed the way to Jesus in that dark prison, just like a flashlight shows us the path where we should walk when it is dark.
3. Explain that Jesus set an example for us to follow—He obeyed His Father in hard times and even in death. God can be trusted to always be with us no matter what. With God as our help and guide, we can know how to choose to follow Jesus. God's presence transforms our choices!
4. Show the secret messages. Part of learning to walk with Jesus is asking the Holy Spirit for help to see things the way He sees them—from His perspective. (Fold the paper and show them the two perspectives.)

Mission Brief Leader Suggested Script:

(Feel free to adapt to your context.)

In our Bible story today, Paul and his friend were beaten for preaching about Jesus. Paul and Silas had learned about Jesus' life. Jesus loved people even when they mistreated Him.

Can anyone tell me how Jesus treated sick people? Do you know how He treated the lepers no one would touch? *(Pause for answers)*
He touched them and healed them.

How did He treat the blind men others made fun of? *(Pause for answers)*
He talked kindly to them and opened their eyes so they could see.

How did He treat the lady caught in the act of sinning? *(Pause for answers)*
He was kind to her. He forgave her and told her she could go and sin no more.

Even when Jesus was dying on the cross, He asked His Father to forgive the people who hurt Him because they didn't understand what they were doing.

Jesus loved people. He healed the sick, touched the untouchable, and fed the hungry. Paul and Silas knew all of this. In prison, after those guards had beaten them and put them in chains and shackles, the Bible says they prayed and worshipped God. There they were—bruised, hurt, and bleeding—and yet they sang and praised God! Paul had learned something…He learned that once we receive Jesus into our lives, we are NEVER alone! We ALWAYS have a Friend, a Comforter in hard times, and a Counselor when we need advice. God was with them in that prison, and they felt His peace even though they were in trouble! They knew God was with them, and they were grateful for His loving presence! They could not stop praising God even in the middle of this difficult situation.

As Paul and Silas were singing and praising God, an earthquake came and shook the prison until all the doors flung open. It even broke off their shackles and their chains fell off. They were free to go! But Paul and Silas knew the jailer would get in big trouble if they left. He would be punished and possibly killed if they escaped. Instead of running away, they did the unthinkable. They stayed right in their prison cell and called out to him so he would not harm himself in his hopelessness. It is amazing what we can do when we stay focused on God and realize we are NOT alone. Jesus is always with us! *When we have Jesus, we have a power that is beyond our own strength. It is a power that helps us do what is right, a power that helps us make wise choices, and a power that helps us worship even in hard times.*

Our Bible verse says, **"He guides the humble in what is right and teaches them his way,"** (Psalm 25:9).

God's ways are not our ways! But God helps us know what His ways are. Just like the light from this flashlight helps us know where to walk to stay on a path in the dark. We need God to teach us His ways and give us power to walk in His ways. It did not seem to make sense that God would have Paul and Silas stay put in jail, did it? But Jesus knew there was a man there, the jailer, who needed to meet Jesus that day, too!

It is all a matter of how we see things. It is a matter of perspective. *(Start folding Mission Brief Day 3 sheet. Fold along the lines to find the messages on the page. Turn it the other way and see that there are two messages on this one page!)*

Paul could have seen himself in jail from an earthly view. *(Show the Stage 1 side: "I'm in prison and hopeless!")*

But because Paul walked so closely with God, he came to see even this really hard situation from another perspective—from God's perspective! *(Show the Stage 2 side: "Praise God! He is always with me!")*

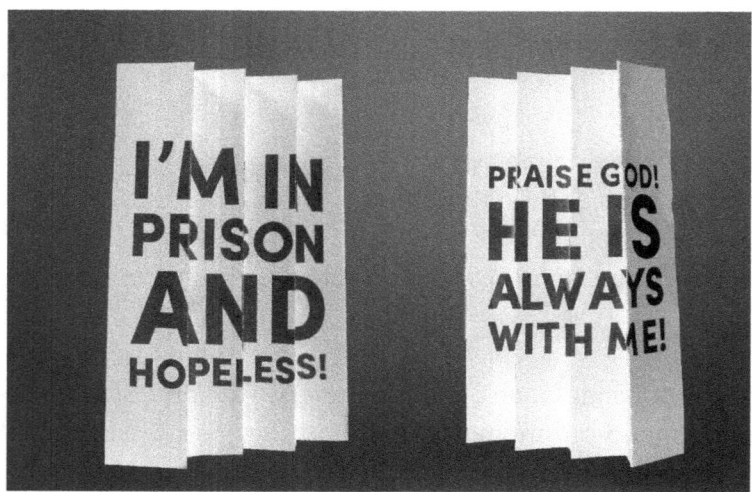

Folded Stage 1: I'm in prison and hopeless!

Folded Stage 2: Praise God! He is always with me!

Jesus' power enables us to see things from HIS perspective!

Raise your hand if you have ever met someone who is not a very kind person. I think if Paul and Silas did not have Jesus in their life, they would *only* see a mean, cruel jailer. They would not have seen him as someone who needed Jesus, too! When we keep our eyes on Jesus and walk with Him, His presence helps us see the world from His perspective. Just like a flashlight transforms the dark and helps us see things that we could not see before. With Jesus' presence, we have the power to love people and treat people the way Jesus wants us to. **Jesus' presence transforms our choices,** just like it did for Paul. Jesus loved that jailer. Because Paul and Silas chose to worship God when things got hard, the jailer's life and the lives of his whole family were transformed! So when we're wondering what we should do, simply ask God to show us His perspective. Think about a flashlight and ask ourselves, "How would Jesus see these people and handle this situation?"

DAY THREE

Transformation Station

EVIDENCE VAULT: PSALM 25:9

Play the theme song or memory verse song as children enter the room. Open your time with the top secret hand signal.

Supplies:
- Recording of the day's **memory verse song**
- **Memory verse chart**
- Optional **prizes or mission money**
- **Supplies for memory verse game** from the resource section of nazarene.org/vbs

Mission Brief Leader Suggested Script:

Who remembers today's secret passcode? *(Pause for answers)*
Jesus' presence transforms my choices!

Our verse today helps us better understand how the passcode works.

Psalm 25:9
"He guides the humble in what is right and teaches them his way."

Remember yesterday when we talked about listening to Jesus' voice? *(Review "My sheep listen to my voice…," John 10:27.)*

Today's Bible verse shows us how we can know what is right. God Himself guides us in what is right and teaches us His way.

What does this verse mean?

Someone who is humble does not think of themselves as the most important. They are not proud. They are respectful and choose to submit to God. We do not hear "submit" very often in our world. Submit means to allow someone else to be in charge. Most people want to be the boss; not many people see the importance of being a good follower, someone who obeys well.

Of course, we do not follow just anyone; that would be foolish! This verse helps us know why it is important to allow God to be in charge of our life. God loves us and we can trust Him. When we humble ourselves and trust Him by obeying and following Him, He teaches us and we learn what is right! This verse is so important for us to memorize so we never forget to choose to respect and obey God. Then we will learn what is right and God will teach us His way!

> **BONUS VERSE:** **1 Timothy 6:18**
>
> "Command them to do good, to be rich in good deeds, and to be generous and willing to share."

Closing

Outline the plan your church has made to reward children that memorize Scripture this week. A downloadable memory verse chart is provided for you to write the children's names and keep track of who has memorized which verses. Allow them time each day to repeat them to you.

Go over the memory verse several times.

If they are ready, have children come to you individually to say their verse. Mark it on the memory verse chart. If you are giving prizes or secret mission money for saying today's portion of the verse, hand them out now.

If time allows, play a memory verse game from the memory verse games resource.

DAY THREE

Transformation Station

CRAFT LAB: INVISIBLE INK

Play the theme song and the memory verse song as children arrive. Ask the children to repeat the memory verse or the passcode for the day.

Supplies:
- **Paper**
- **Pens**
- **Cotton swabs**
- **Lemon juice**
- **Blow dryer, hot light bulb, or a hot oven and a cookie sheet**

Directions:

Pass out paper and a cotton swab to each child. Have children write a secret message or draw a simple smiley face on their paper with lemon juice and the cotton swab and set aside to dry.

Ask to see someone's secret message. Take a blow dryer (or a light bulb) to the note. Show the kids the secret message.

Mission Brief Leader Suggested Script:

When we begin a new friendship, we talk a lot to each other. Communication is how we get to know that person better. With God, we communicate to Him through prayer, and we hear from Him through His Word and through His Holy Spirit in us. As we spend more and more time with Him in prayer and in His Word, His presence in our life begins to transform how we think and how we see the world. We realize how much He loves the people He brings across our path. When we see people the way He does, we begin to find ways to share God's love with them. God's presence transforms our choices!

Just as we had to spend some time to heat up this note to reveal the message, we really have to spend time reading the Bible and thinking about what it says to understand God's message to us. We need Him to help us understand what Scripture is telling us about how God wants us to live.

Sometimes God's message is hard to see, like our craft. Sometimes the Bible may seem confusing. We should always talk to God and ask Him to help us understand His Word. Sometimes He sends people who have really studied the Scripture to teach us and help us to understand.

(Twist: Have older kids use their pen to write a note over the secret message to disguise it even more before revealing the hidden message.)

The world often tries to distract us from the message of the Good News of Jesus by telling us it is not real or true, or by keeping us distracted or too busy so we do not read the Bible. What can you do to help you remember to read the Bible? *(Pause for answers)*

(If possible, have Bibles available for children who do not have access to one. Consider providing copies of a Bible reading plan for the children.)

DAY THREE

Transformation Station

**RECHARGE STATION:
PAUL IN PRISON SNACK MIX**

Play the theme song and the memory verse song as children arrive. Ask the children to repeat the memory verse or passcode for the day.

Supplies:
- **A cup or zip top plastic bag**
- **Oyster crackers or small crackers**
- **Mini-marshmallows**
- **M&Ms or chocolate chips**
- **Gummy bears or graham cracker bears**
- **Small pretzel sticks**
- **Nuts.** *Exercise sensitivity to food allergies and eliminate nuts if needed.*

(Substitute fruits and vegetable items for a healthier option.)

Directions:
Today you will retell the story of Paul in prison. At each part of the story, have the children get the snack that goes with that part of the story to create their own snack mix. Let the kids tell as much of the story as they can remember OR you can read the story straight out of **Acts 16:16-34**.

Mission Brief Leader Suggested Script:

Paul and his friend **Silas**	*2 gummy or graham cracker bears*
came into a new town and were walking the **stone roads**, helping people	*A small handful of oyster crackers or small crackers*
when they met a **slave woman** and freed her.	*1 gummy or graham cracker bear*
The townspeople were mad that they freed the slave woman. They beat Paul and Silas and put them in **prison**.	*Several small pretzel sticks*
At midnight, Paul and Silas were **praying and praising God**	*Several M&Ms or chocolate chips and mini marshmallows to represent the sweet songs and prayers that came from Paul and Silas' hearts*
when an **earthquake** shook the ground and the prison doors flew open and chains fell off their feet.	*Nuts to show the ground broke up or crush a couple of crackers*
The **jailer** was so upset and he was going to harm himself, but Paul and Silas said, "Don't hurt yourself! We're all still here!" The jailer realized only God could give these two men such happy hearts and make them this kind. The jailer wanted to know Jesus, too.	*1 gummy or graham cracker bear*
The jailer took them to his own house, bandaged up their wounds, and asked Paul to teach his **whole family** about Jesus. Paul was happy to do this and because of this, all of the jailer's family came to know Jesus, too!	*Several gummy or graham cracker bears*

- What good came out of Paul and Silas being in prison?
- Have you ever seen God change a bad/hard situation into good?
- Share a time when God used a bad situation for good in your own life.
- Discuss how the story might have ended differently if Paul and Silas had acted differently, if they were mad at God or mean to the jailer.
- What if Paul, Silas, and the other prisoners had run away after the earthquake?
- How can we trust God when things look hard or difficult?

Closing:
If time allows, have the kids review the passcode, the verse with motions, and songs.

DAY THREE

Transformation Station

AGENT TRAINING FIELD: I KNOW MY SHOE!

Equipment:
None (other than the shoes on the children's feet)

Objective:
To be the first team to retrieve all their shoes

How to Play the Game:
Begin by having all children remove their shoes and toss them into a pile at the opposite end of the room or yard. Have your helper mix up the shoes and push them together to form a tight pile.

Based on the number of children at your VBS, divide them into equal teams (two to four teams with no more than eight to a team). Line the kids up at the starting line (relay style).

When you blow your whistle, the first child from each team will race to the shoe pile and find one of their missing shoes. Once a shoe is found, they must put it on, race back, and tag the next person in line. The relay continues until one team collects all their shoes and returns to the starting line with everybody seated.

Small Group Alternative:
Have a few helpers collect all the shoes and hide them around the room or yard. Make sure the kids do not watch them hide the shoes! Split into equal teams of two to four kids (per team) and have them search together for their shoes. The first team to find all their teams' shoes is the winner!

Memory Verse Application:

How did you know which shoe was yours? *(Pause for answers)*
I've had it for a year. I knew it was mine because the shoe lace was broken on one side.

We know our shoes because we spend a LOT of time with our shoes. They go with us everywhere we go. We know them because we have a history with them.

Remember our memory verse for today? **"He guides the humble in what is right and teaches them his way" (Psalm 25:9).**

The more we walk with God and spend time with Him, the more we recognize Him and see Him at work in the world.

Did anyone have a hard time finding his or her shoe? How long ago did you get that shoe? *(Pause for answers. Hopefully they are new and they could not quite remember what their shoe looked like.)*

Sometimes we do not see God working because we have not spent much time with Him, just like that new shoe that was hard to find. If you cannot see God's work in your life yet, just keep spending time with Him, with the Bible, His Word, and with His people. The more time you spend with Him, the more you will recognize Him and His voice.

If you have never asked Jesus to give you new life, today would be the perfect day to give your heart to Him and start that lifelong friendship!

DAY THREE

Transformation Station

INFILTRATION SERVICE PROJECT

Allow the children to be a help and a friend to someone because Jesus is our Help and Friend.

Remember:

Remind the children that Jesus' loving presence transforms our choices. Jesus is always with us. He equips us with wisdom and provides for our needs. Because our needs are cared for, we can help others with their needs. Remember when Paul was in jail? Paul kept his mind on God and sang praises even though he was in the dark and cold. Because Paul had a heart for God, he could look past his own situation and help the jailer understand that God loved him and wanted him to be saved. Our scripture says, **"He guides the humble in what is right and teaches them his way" (Psalm 25:9)**. God helps us to see opportunities to give Him praise in every situation. He will give us wisdom and strength, especially in uncomfortable situations. He is our help and guide.

Ideas:

- Help sort food in the church's food pantry.
- Be a friend to the elderly who attend your church by making cards, making a beautiful sign, coloring pictures, or making a craft to give them.
- Prepare dry soup mixes in jars or zip top plastic bags to give to the hungry. The ingredients could be donated prior to VBS by church members.
- Support a local charity. This could be filling backpacks for children with school supplies donated by church members or organizing clothes for a clothing closet.

DAY THREE

Closing Skit

Play theme song and memory verse song as children return.

Ask volunteers to share the passcode, memory verse, favorite activity, or something they learned. Or have trivia questions prepared to ask early arrivers.

Begin with the top secret hand signal.

Dialogue:

Director: What a great day we had learning that **Jesus' presence transforms my choices!** Let's welcome back our worship leader to review our two songs for today.

(Worship leader sings theme song and today's memory verse song with hand motions.)

(Agent Strange is hidden where kids can see him, but Tre and Buddy cannot. Agent Tre comes limping in, obviously in a lot of pain with a bandage on his leg or foot.)

Agent Tre: *(Limps in singing today's song)*

    Buddy: *(Upset, interrupts Tre)* How can you be singing? Aren't you angry? You know who set that trap for you, don't you?

Agent Tre: Yes, I do.

    Agent Strange: *(Looks shocked)*

    Buddy: He meant to hurt you, and that makes me mad! Can I do anything for you? Do you need any help? *(Pulling up a chair to rest Tre's leg on)* Are you sure you're going to be all right?

Agent Tre: I'll be OK, Buddy. I know Strange is always trying to trip me up, but I also know why. His dad was a really good special agent and Strange wants to be one too. He just doesn't know how because he still doesn't understand.

    Agent Strange: *(Looking shocked and surprised that Tre knows this)*

Agent Tre: Strange doesn't understand that being an agent is not about who your parents are or what you're like on the outside. It's about having a real relationship with Jesus. He's the Boss because He's our Savior. Strange wants to be an agent more than anything, but he's going about it the wrong way.

    Agent Strange: *(Looks very sad)*

Buddy: Agent Tre, something is really bothering me.

Agent Tre: What's that, Buddy?

Buddy: When your leg got caught in that trap, I could tell you were hurt, and I heard you pray for the Boss to send help. I kept waiting for someone to show up, but I finally couldn't stand it any longer so I helped you myself.

Agent Tre: *(Laughing)* Oh, Buddy! Don't you see? He DID send help!

Buddy: *(Upset)* He did not! It was just us! The two of us! Nobody else! He didn't answer your prayer! He never sent anybody!

Agent Tre: Wait a minute, Buddy. When I couldn't free myself from that trap, who was there to help me? You were! Who helped me back to the car? You did! And who stopped the bleeding until we made it to the hospital? Mister B-U-Double-D-Y, that's who! When I was in serious trouble, God sent YOU, Buddy.

Buddy: *(Surprised and so pleased)* Wow! I guess I didn't think about it like that. Agent Tre, I have another confession to make. Do you remember on the first day of *Operation Transformation* how I prayed and asked God to transform my heart? I wanted to be an agent because I wanted to be like you, with your cool clothes, great gadgets, and exciting adventures. But the more I've hung around you, the more I've realized how awesome the Boss is! Now I want to be an agent because I want to know Him like you do! I want to be able to live for Him like you!

Agent Tre: I'm glad to hear that, Buddy! And I'm not at all surprised. Buddy, God has been at work transforming you ever since you prayed on that first day. You have been listening to His voice all week and learning more about Him every day. I can tell that you have been hungry to know Him better. Your desire reflects today's memory verse. **Psalm 25:9** says, **"He guides the humble in what is right and teaches them His way."** You are learning His way and doing the next right thing. It's no longer all about you, it's all about Him. That is AWESOME, Buddy!

Buddy: But how can I be sure I'm getting it right, Tre? I'm so scared I'm going to mess up and choose the wrong things.

Agent Tre: Do you have a copy of the Agent Handbook yet?

Buddy: Well no. Is that something I have to have special training to read?

Agent Tre: No, Buddy, anyone can read it. The more you read it, the better you will know the Boss and how He wants us to live. But Buddy, listen to me. This is important. God's not looking for perfect performance. He's looking for honest, sincere hearts and minds that are fully devoted to Him. You're doing just fine, partner. As a matter of fact, if you will come with me I have a copy of the Handbook just for you! *(Puts his arm around his shoulder and they both walk off together)*

Agent Strange: *(Waits for them to walk off the stage, looks sad, and walks off the stage, too)*

Director: God has given us another great day at *Operation Transformation!* Each day we have more to celebrate! While you were in your Transformation Stations, we counted the offering. Do you want to know who gave the most today, the girls or the boys?

The girls gave $_____ and the boys gave $_____! Way to go!

It is time to stand for our closing prayer: Thank You, God, for your transforming love for each one of us. Thank You for the chance to learn more about you and the chance to help other children around the world. We pray that you will help other children know Your love and Your Son, Jesus! Amen.

Everyone take off your nametags and give them to your group leader. You can pick them up when you come back tomorrow. Okay? And everybody remember to bring a friend, so they can hear about *Operation Transformation* too!

Closing:

Give any other announcements or direction for dismissal. Play theme song as children leave.

OPERATION TRANSFORMATION

DAY FOUR

DAY FOUR

Table of Contents

Week at a Glance 4

Leadership Meeting 6

Opening & Welcome 8

Opening Skit 10

Transformation Stations 14
    Mission Brief 14
    Evidence Vault 18
    Craft Lab 20
    Recharge Station 22
    Agent Training Field 24
    Infiltration Service Project 26

Closing Skit 27

DAY FOUR

Leadership Meeting

- Greeting and appreciation
- Our goal is to *help kids experience life-transforming encounters with Jesus Christ.*
- Review training meeting highlights (bathroom policy, safety policy, discipline, what to do in case of illness or emergency, releasing children at day's end, etc.). Since the details were provided at a prior training, offer these on a single printed page as a reminder.
- Remind leaders of the special offering project.

Day 4 Overview:

Today's Passcode:	Today's Theology Focus:	Today's Bible Story:
Jesus' call transforms my mission	**Sending** Use every opportunity to weave this into your time with the kids.	**Acts 22:1-16** (read aloud)

Review Today's Memory Verse:

John 17:3a
"Now this is eternal life: that they know you, the only true God, and Jesus Christ…"

Review Top Secret Hand Signal:

Tap-tap, clap-clap, snap-snap, SHHHHHH!

Pat palms on top of legs two times, clap hands two times, snap fingers two times, and place finger to lips while shushing. NOTE: some people have difficulty snapping their fingers; encourage them to close all four fingers onto their palms.

- Review today's songs. Motions to John 17:3a are included on the media section of nazarene.org/vbs.
- Review today's schedule.
- Questions, comments, or concerns?
- Close with prayer at least 15 minutes before start time.

OUR PRAYER FOR YOU:

Father God, we worship You for Who You are.

There is no one like You, Who loves, seeks, and saves the lost.

All of our preparation has brought us to this moment.

Now, Father, bring the children You know need to be here today.

Cut out all distractions so the Good News will go forth without hindrance.

Give us ears to hear Your Spirit and the right words to communicate Your love to the children.

Help us remember what we have prepared to present to the children today.

Give us the energy and enthusiasm to make Your Word

as exciting, engaging, and powerful as it truly is.

We pray the children will fall in love with You and with Your Word.

Draw them by Your grace into a right relationship with you.

Grant us strength to carry out Your work here today.

Protect these kids and these workers.

Take care of our families at home while we seek to expand your Kingdom here.

May Your Kingdom come and Your will be done here today.

We will be careful to give You all the glory.

In Jesus' name and for the sake of His Kingdom,

Amen.

DAY FOUR

Opening & Welcome

Be prepared to transition quickly from music to dialogue to music to skit to keep attention focused.

Sing Theme Song and Day 1, 2, and 3 Songs with Hand Motions

Starting with music engages everyone's attention and participation.

Welcome

The following is a suggested script:

Director: Welcome to Day Four of *Operation Transformation!* I am Special Agent _____ and it is so great to see all of you today! I have been looking forward to seeing you and going on our mission today. We are going to have a great day! Did you remember our Bible verse for the week? *(Say the verse you just sang.)*

We have already learned three other verses. Who knows John 1:12? *(Pause for answers)*

Does anyone remember our passcode for Day 1? It has something to do with becoming children of God…*(Pause for answers)*
That is right! "Jesus' love transforms my identity!"

On Day 2 we learned about hearing God's voice and that His power transforms us when we follow Him. Who can remember our verse, John 10:27? *(Pause for answers)*

Does anyone remember the passcode from yesterday? Paul demonstrated this even when his circumstances were bad. *(Pause for answers)*
That's right! "Jesus' presence transforms my choices!"

How about the verse from yesterday? *(Pause for answers)*
Psalm 25:9 says, "He guides the humble in what is right and teaches them his way." You have really been paying attention!

We have had a great week so far, and it is not over yet! We are in for another great day together! Paul went on many great adventures with God. Today we are going to hear as Paul thinks back over his life and celebrates how God called him and transformed Paul's mission. God was faithful to provide for Paul's needs throughout his life. Through Paul's life, we have seen God's transforming love and power over and over. As Paul remembers, he realizes how God's call to follow Him put Paul on a special journey, a mission from God Himself. Which brings us to our passcode for today, **"Jesus' call transforms my mission."** Say it with me, **"Jesus' call transforms my mission!"** Let's hear the boys!…Let's hear the girls!…Now all together! **"Jesus' call transforms my mission!"**

We also have a new verse today that helps us on our mission of sharing the Good News! **John 17:3a** says, **"Now this is eternal life: that they know you, the only true God, and Jesus Christ…"** Paul's mission was to share this good news with the world. This is also the ultimate mission for us to share today.

Offering

Director: As we receive our offering today, we are going to sing this verse and learn the motions. But before we do, who can share what our offering project is for this week? *(Share about your mission project for those who may be new. You can find information about the Kids Reaching Kids Offering at nazarene.org/sdmi.)*

That's right. So far you have given $_____ towards our project. We are going to sing our new verse for the day and learn the motions while you bring your offering. Don't worry if you don't have anything to give today, follow your leader anyway. Now that you know, you can bring it on Sunday when we share all we have learned with our parents. Today, we will all meet back here before going home and that's when we'll see if the GIRLS or BOYS won!

(Play today's memory verse song and receive the offering. Use this time to make any other special announcements. When everyone has returned to their seats, lead them in the top secret hand signal to get their attention.)

Great job everyone! You just heard today's memory verse song. We'll be singing it all day—but of course we need to learn it first! So let's sing it one more time before we meet Agent Tre and Buddy to find out about today's mission.

Sing Theme Song with Hand Motions

Sing Day 4 Song with Hand Motions

DAY FOUR

Opening Skit

Props & Characters:

- **Special agent lockbox**, marked "Top Secret"
- 1 cross
- 1-2 chairs
- 1 watch
- NIV Bible
- **Special Agent Tre** (Code Name: Trinity); dressed like a spy, with a hat and sunglasses
- **Special Agent Buddy** (Code Name: Barnabas); dressed identical to Tre
- **Agent Strange/Scout**

Note: Use any additional props available to increase interest. Encourage the characters to move often and to use the whole platform/stage.

Dialogue:

Agent Tre: *(Practicing John 17:3a to himself)* **"Now this is eternal life: that they know you, the only true God, and Jesus Christ..." (John 17:3a).** I need to get this right for tonight's commissioning ceremony. "Now this is eternal life..." *(Phone rings, Tre answers)* **Jesus' call transforms my mission.** Agent Trinity speaking. Yes sir. Of course, sir. Do You want me to wait for Buddy...I mean Agent Buddy? No? Ok, I will head right out. Thank You, sir. *(Tre exits stage)*

Agent Buddy: *(Enters opposite side of stage)* Agent Tre? Kids, have you seen Agent Tre? What? He was just here? That's weird; he usually waits for me. Oh, well. I'll just wait here for him.

Hey recruits! I've got something to show you! *(Sits down, removes his shoe and places it to his ear)* Dial tone! And that's not all! *(Jumps up and goes over to the special agent lockbox)* Check this out! *(Opens lockbox with thumbprint and proudly holds up the cross and Bible.)*

Agent Tre: *(Re-enters stage)*

Agent Buddy: Agent Tre! Look! I can open the special agent lockbox! I can hardly believe it. I really am a special agent. Well, almost. I know it's not official until the ceremony, but still—this is AWESOME!

(Agent Strange enters same side as Tre)

Agent Buddy: What is HE doing here?

Agent Tre: Agent Buddy, this is Scout. *(Awkward moment as Buddy glares at Scout, who looks down at the floor)* Have a seat and make yourself comfortable, Scout. *(Scout sits down, now even more nervous. Buddy pulls Tre to the other side of the stage for a "private" talk.)*

Agent Buddy: *(In a loud stage whisper)* Are you serious? Why would you bring him here? You know he can't be trusted! Yesterday he trapped you, the day before he tricked you—or tried to…

Agent Tre: Agent Buddy, when the Boss gives us a mission, what are we supposed to do?

Agent Buddy: Carry it out. Follow wherever He leads us.

Agent Tre: That's right! Well, He gave me a mission this morning: to bring Agent Strange—I mean Scout—back here. So that's what I did. Whatever the Boss has in mind, there's one thing I know: everyone needs the Lord, Buddy. Even Scout! If I recall, it wasn't too long ago that you didn't have a relationship with Jesus either.

Scout: So, uh, thanks for inviting me into your headquarters and all, but why am I here? What exactly do you want from me?

Agent Tre: Oh, I don't want anything FROM you, Scout. I was wondering if I could do anything FOR you.

Scout: What???

Agent Tre: Well, I don't really know you, but I know the Boss really loves you and…

Scout: *(Stands up, suddenly angry)* Stop right there! I am out of here! *(Starts walking away)*

Agent Tre: What? Wait! Did I say something wrong?

Scout: Yeah! You did! *(Turns and faces Tre)* You said the Boss loves me but that can't be true. I've tried and tried to be good enough, but I always fall short. *(Tre and Buddy look at each other, confused)*

Agent Tre: What makes you say that?

Scout: My dad was an awesome agent—you've even said so yourself! So I've tried to do all the things I saw my dad do, only better, but it just seems like no matter how hard I try, I always mess things up.

Agent Buddy: Scout, I've got to be honest. When I first started coming here, I just liked the cool gadgets Agent Tre had and the exciting missions he went on. I thought if I could just be like him, I would become an agent too. I started dressing like him and acting like him but that's all it was—an act! I was no different on the inside. That's when I realized that becoming an agent is about being transformed on the INSIDE, not changing what I look like or act like on the outside. But as hard as I tried, I could never change who I was on the inside. I just didn't have the power to do that. And I still don't—but God does! He made real transformation possible through Jesus. Jesus is the key! That's why Jesus IS the Way! Real transformation only happens through a real relationship with Jesus.

Scout: Then I guess I'm just hopeless. *(Starts for the door)*

Agent Buddy: I get that. *(Scout pauses)* I understand how you feel because that's what I believed too. I thought following Jesus meant you would suddenly have it all together and never mess up again. Then I realized that didn't make any sense. Jesus' disciples certainly didn't have it all together. They messed up, too. But something WAS different about Jesus AND His followers. They were different on the inside, which changed how they responded on the outside. They really were transformed. Take Agent Paul and Silas, for instance. They were unfairly beaten and imprisoned, and yet they still had joy. Following Jesus doesn't mean I'll never mess up or that I won't experience consequences, or hard times. It means that I can have joy deep inside even when bad things happen, because I'm never alone. Jesus is right there with me.

Agent Tre: Thanks, Buddy. I couldn't have said it better myself. Hey, Scout! We're having a special agent commissioning service for Buddy. I'd love for you to be there if you can make it. Oh! One last thing before you head out. I wanted you to have this. *(Takes out the watch purchased during the earlier mission and hands it to him.)*

Scout: *(Scout looks at it in shock; voice gets shaky)* Wh-where…did…you get this?!

Agent Tre: The Boss sent us on a mission to find it. He didn't tell us why. We looked all over the city for it. Just now, I got the clear impression that I was supposed to give it to YOU.

Scout: This is just like my dad's watch. I don't know what else to say but thank you! I, uh, I'll think about what you said, Buddy. And maybe I will be at that service. I don't know. I've got a lot to think about. *(Scout leaves. Tre and Buddy look at each other.)*

Agent Tre: I had no idea that watch would mean so much to him.

Agent Buddy: I think it's awesome being an agent for a Boss who loves people so much!

Agent Tre: And I really appreciate how you told your story, Buddy. That's exactly what Agent Paul did. When people are hurting, they often get angry and they can lash out. They might even want to argue about God and Jesus. But when we just share the facts about what Jesus did for us and how we were transformed when we chose to follow Him, there's nothing to argue about because it's the obvious truth!

Agent Buddy: *(Beaming)* Oh, almost forgot! My thumbprint worked and THIS was in the special agent lockbox! *(Holds up the cross)* Do you know what it means?

Agent Tre: Nope. I guess we'll have to find that out in our Mission Brief! In the meantime, let's get ready for your commissioning ceremony! Recruits, you're all invited to Buddy's commissioning too. We'll see you after your Transformation Stations!

Director: I wonder if Scout is going to be all right. I sure hope so! Isn't it something how the Boss spoke to Tre about giving Scout that watch? I can't wait until Buddy's special ceremony. I'm so glad we are all invited to celebrate. Wow! We have a big day ahead! I'll be sure to take the cross to your Mission Brief Station so you can figure out how it relates to today's mission!

Closing:

If time allows, sing 1-2 songs focused on Jesus our King; our obedience; God's call.

End with Day 4 Song, *"John 17:3a, Now this is eternal life,"* with hand motions.

Kids are dismissed by groups and given any instructions they need to get to their Transformation Station.

Play theme song as children exit.

DAY FOUR

Transformation Station

**MISSION BRIEF:
A TALE OF TWO BALLOONS!**

Preparation:
- If possible, the leader should wear a **white lab coat**.
- Prepare a **large manila envelope** with "MISSION BRIEF #4" written in large letters on the outside. Place a copy of the **script** inside.
- A **small cross**, like the one in the lockbox from the opening skit.
- Have a **current NIV Bible** with your supplies.
- **2 balloons**, identical in color and size. Fill one with helium and fill one with air. Draw identical faces on each with a marker. (Hide these two balloons while you review the previous lessons.)

Directions:
Play the song for today's verse as children arrive and leave. Have the two balloons hidden while you review previous lessons. Do not let the children see that they are different in any way.

As you teach the lesson, hold one balloon in each hand at the base so they each stand upright.

Review:

Day 1: **Jesus' love transforms my identity.**
How is our white flower today?

(Emphasize the fact that the more we spend time with God in prayer, reading the Bible, and learning from other Christians, the more we look like Jesus. The more time the flower spends in the colored water, the more it looks like the colored water.)

Day 2: **Jesus' power transforms my life.**
What is caterpillar soup and what does it have to do with Jesus' power to transform my life?

Caterpillars completely dissolve into a "caterpillar soup" in their cocoons and are totally transformed, literally re-made into butterflies, just like we are when Jesus comes to live inside us! He changes our focus. We become a part of His family with a new identity. As we trust and follow Him, He transforms us as our faith in Him gets stronger.

Day 3: **Jesus' presence transforms my choices.**
Who remembers what we learned in our Mission Brief yesterday?

Because Paul kept his eyes on God, he chose to praise God even though he was in jail. It would have been easy for Paul to look only at his circumstances and be sad because he had been beaten and was now in jail for doing nothing wrong. Because of his choice to praise God, Paul was able to share the good news with the jailer and the jailer's whole family was saved. We also talked about growing closer to Jesus by reading the Bible and praying or talking to Him. We learned that the Holy Spirit helps us to understand the Bible and to see things from God's perspective!

Mission Brief Summary:

(Feel free to make this your own!)

1. Tell the story outlined in **Acts 22:1-16**. Paul shares his story with the crowd. (Jesus' call transformed Paul's mission.)
2. Explain that Paul had known it might be dangerous to go to Jerusalem, but he also knew that God had called him to go there. His relationship with Jesus had sustained him through hard times before. Paul wanted to share with the crowd all that God had done for him and through his obedience.
3. Explain that Paul wanted to be sure that everyone knew that God had transformed his identity, his life, and his choices. God had called him to bring the Good News of Jesus' love (represented by the cross) to a group of people that he understood best. God had totally transformed Paul's mission from persecuting Christians to encouraging Jews to become new Christians who were free from their old ways and free to accept Jesus and His mission.
4. When it is time to let the balloons go, they show that when we accept Jesus as our Savior, we are free to be all He created us to be—agents of His love in a hurting world—rather than continuing to be burdened and weighed down by our guilt and shame. As we share our story of His transforming love at work in us, others will be challenged to look up and see our changed life, and His transforming power will begin to work in them as well.

Mission Brief Leader Suggested Script:

(Feel free to adapt to your context.)

Wherever Paul went, they discouraged him. Sometimes they put him in prison and beat him for preaching about Jesus. In our story today, Paul had gone to Jerusalem. Some Jewish leaders had stirred up a great riot, saying Paul was a trouble-maker. The mob of people got so angry that they were determined to kill Paul. When the Roman soldiers heard about the riot, they immediately came and arrested Paul. When they asked the crowd what Paul had done, the crowd became so wild that the soldiers actually had to carry Paul away. As they were taking him away, Paul asked to speak to the crowd. The commander let Paul stand on the steps so all the people could see him. Then Paul did something so strange! He spoke to the crowd in a different language so he could get their attention. They all listened closely while Paul told the crowd his whole story!

Paul told of how he grew up and that he was taught by the best teachers. He shared that he was a good student and followed all the Jewish laws. *(Ask the children if anyone can help by telling what they remember learning about Saul on the first day. Pause for answers.)*

Paul said something like, "I used to believe exactly what you believe. I used to persecute Christians, putting them in jail and even killing them." Then he told them about what happened on the road to Damascus. *(Ask for a volunteer to tell what happened.)*

A bright light blinded him. Saul heard Jesus' voice and followed His instructions. He told them about Ananias, who prayed for him, and after that prayer, he could see again. Then he told them what Ananias said to him that day. "The God of our ancestors has chosen you…You will be his witness to all people of what you have seen and heard. *(Hold up the cross)* And now what are you waiting for? Get up, be baptized and wash your sins away, calling on his name" (Acts 22:14-16).

Whenever Paul had the chance to speak to someone, he told this story! He told of how he came to know Jesus was real. *(Hold up the cross.)* This cross can always remind us that Jesus is real and His love for everyone is real. Paul told everyone how they could come to know Jesus…"Get up, be baptized and wash your sins away, calling on his name."

It was Jesus' call that transformed Paul's mission! Paul was on a mission to stop Christianity. When Jesus called Paul, suddenly his life mission was totally changed.

Do you see these two balloons? They represent two people. One of these people knows and follows Jesus. One does not. Can you tell which one is a Jesus follower just by looking at them? They both have happy smiles on their faces.

But one of them is filled with something special. When we become a Christian, we realize we have disobeyed God (we have sinned) and we tell Him we are sorry. We ask Him to forgive us and wash away our sins. We are free from our old way of thinking. We are free to understand God more clearly and to think about how He wants us to live. We then have room in our hearts for Him to come in and live inside. The Holy Spirit, the Counselor and Comforter we talked about yesterday, comes to be our Forever Friend and we never have to be alone again. He fills us up with God's love and His presence. He fills us with wisdom and understanding about how to live in a way that will please God.

(Let go of both balloons. One will rise to the ceiling. The other will fall flat.)

THIS is why Paul spent the rest of his life telling people about Jesus! He wanted all of us to know the truth he found…that Jesus is real and His love for us is powerful! That Jesus had come to set us free from our sin and disobedience and set us free to be what God had created us to be, His special agents in the world. Agent Paul wanted everyone to hear this good news.

You see, Jesus' call in Paul's life transformed his mission, and when Jesus comes into OUR lives, we want to share this amazing Friend with others, too!

It is as easy as doing what Paul did, telling our story of how Jesus has come in our hearts to be our Friend! We want everyone to be filled with His Spirit and to be set free to carry on God's mission of telling others the good news of Jesus *(Point to the helium balloon).*

(Invite any who want to share their story of accepting Jesus to share. Ask if anyone wants to accept Jesus' free gift of salvation. If so, use the Leading a Child to Christ document from the resource section of nazarene.org/vbs. Be sure to share with a child's leader if a child accepts Christ as their Savior so that they can share this news with the child's parent.)

DAY FOUR

Transformation Station

EVIDENCE VAULT: JOHN 17:3a

Play the theme song or memory verse song as children enter the room. Open your time with the top secret hand signal.

Supplies:

- Recording of the day's **memory verse song**
- **Memory verse chart**
- Optional **prizes or mission money**
- **Supplies for memory verse game** from the resource section of nazarene.org/vbs

Evidence Vault Leader Suggested Script:

We have learned a lot of great verses this week. Who can name a verse you have learned? *(Pause for answers)*

Try to review each verse so far.

Who remembers today's secret passcode? *(Pause for answers)*
Jesus' call transforms my mission!

Our verse today helps us better understand what mission the passcode is talking about. Our verse is:

John 17:3a
"Now this is eternal life: that they know you, the only true God, and Jesus Christ…"

According to our verse, what do you think the mission is? *(Pause for answers)*

What does this verse mean? *(Pause for answers)*

John tells us how we can have eternal life or life forever—by knowing the one true God and His Son, Jesus.

God loves us so much that He sent His own Son to make forgiveness possible. John 3:16 says that God loved us so much that He sent His one and only Son into the world so that through believing in Him, the world would have eternal life with God. On the first day of VBS, we talked about the importance of receiving the gift He gave and believing in His name. We said that if we do this, we are adopted into God's FAMILY! He gives us the right to become children of God! That is what our verse said in John 1:12, "Yet to all who did receive him, to those who believed in his name, he gave the right to become children of God...." Today's verse says that the way to eternal life is to KNOW the only true God and His Son, Jesus Christ.

When we say we know the only true God and His Son, Jesus, we are not just saying we know ABOUT God. We are talking about having a real relationship with God. Like you know your very best friend. You know their voice because they are familiar to you. You have spent time with them. It's not just knowing about someone, like a movie star that you recognize on TV. This is knowing someone because you have a friendship with them. Jesus is one friend you can always count on to be with you. Jesus is never too busy for you. He will always listen to you and He is always speaking to us through the Bible, through His Spirit, and other Christians.

BONUS VERSE: Psalm 46:1

"God is our refuge and strength, an ever-present help in trouble."

Closing

Outline the plan your church has made to reward children that memorize Scripture this week. A downloadable memory verse chart is provided for you to write the children's names and keep track of who has memorized which verses. Allow them time each day to repeat them to you.

Go over the memory verse several times.

If they are ready, have children come to you individually to say their verse. Mark it on the memory verse chart. If you are giving prizes or secret mission money for saying today's portion of the verse, hand them out now.

If time allows, play a memory verse game from the memory verse games resource.

DAY FOUR

Transformation Station

CRAFT LAB: SALVATION BRACELET

Play the theme song and the memory verse song as children arrive. Ask the children to repeat the memory verse or the passcode for the day.

Supplies:

- **Salvation Bracelet Kit**
    - One of each: black, red, blue, white, green, and yellow bead for each child
    - Strip of leather, shoestring, or thin, black elastic long enough for the child's wrist with enough room to tie knots to hold the beads in place.

Directions:

Give each child the pre-sorted materials for the craft. If possible, place beads and string in a zip top plastic bag for each child prior to class. Lead the children through the directions of making the bracelet with the colors in this order: black, red, blue, white, green, and yellow. As you make the bracelets, share with the children what each color represents.

Craft Lab Leader Suggested Script:

We can tell our story many different ways. Today we will do a craft to help us tell our story to others!

The black bead represents sin. Sin is disobeying God. Everyone has sinned. Sin separates us from God (Romans 3:23).

The red bead represents love. God loved us so much that He made a way for us to not stay stuck in our sin (John 3:16 or 1 John 4:9).

The blue bead reminds us of the water used in baptism. Baptism is a sign that our sins have been washed away (Acts 2:38 and 41).

The white bead represents our sins being forgiven. When you ask Jesus to forgive your sins, your heart is clean (Psalm 51:7 or 1 John 3:5).

The green bead reminds of things that grow. We want to continue a vibrant relationship with God as we read God's Word and learn to follow Him (2 Peter 3:18).

The yellow bead represents heaven. God has given us eternal life and prepared a place called heaven where there are streets of gold (1 John 5:12).

You can use this bracelet to tell other people about Jesus, just like Paul wanted everyone to know what Jesus had done for him. He wanted them to have the same joy of knowing Jesus as he had experienced.

Is telling others about your faith easy?

How will your friends, family, and neighbors hear about Jesus' love unless someone tells them?

(Form pairs and give children a chance to practice by telling each other the story of God's love using their bracelets.)

DAY FOUR

Transformation Station

RECHARGE STATION: POPCORN TRANSFORMATION

Play the theme song and the memory verse song as children arrive. Ask the children to repeat the memory verse or passcode for the day.

Supplies:
- **Kernels of popcorn** (un-popped)
- **Popped corn** (If possible, have popped popcorn already divided into bagged portions for each child).

Recharge Station Leader Suggested Script

Who likes popcorn?

Today we are going to eat some yummy popcorn for our snacks!

(Hand the children each several unpopped kernels of corn and hear the groans.)

We have been talking all week about TRANSFORMATION.

Who can tell me a transformation story we have heard this week while I pass out the popcorn that has already been transformed into the yummy stuff we can eat?

Whenever you eat popcorn, I want you to remember that God can change hard hearts, like Saul's, from the inside out!

Saul's story reminds me of this popcorn.
- He started out with a hard heart like this hard kernel of corn.
- It takes heat to transform this popcorn from the inside out.
- It took Jesus' love to transform Saul from hating Jesus to giving his whole life to serve Jesus.
- Jesus offers His love and forgiveness to each of us sitting around the table today!
- Think of the amazing things God might do with each of you as you give your life to follow Jesus!
  - Can you imagine how amazing our world will be if each one of you will learn to be kind to people like Jesus was? Can you think of someone you can be kind to? *(Let the children share)*
  - You might be a doctor helping heal people, like Jesus did. Or, you might be a president or leader who prays for and serves our country. You might be a teacher who gets to love children and speak truth into their lives. Or, you might be a mommy or daddy that gets to teach your children how to trust Jesus. What would you like to be when you grow up and how might you serve God doing that job? *(Let the children share)*
- God changed the world through Paul and God can change the world through YOU!

(As you eat popcorn, ask questions to engage the kids in Paul's life; review the various parts of this week's lessons. Let them have a chance to process what they have learned by asking questions.)

Closing:
If time allows, have the kids review the passcode, the verse with motions, and songs.

DAY FOUR

Transformation Station

**AGENT TRAINING FIELD:
HELPER AND FRIEND
(3-LEGGED RACE)**

Equipment:
Rope, bandana, cloth, or some other way to tie the middle legs together for the race

Objective:
Be the first pair to reach the end of the race by working together and running in sync with the two legs tied together.

How to Play the Game:
Begin by having the children pair off (preferably girls with girls, and boys with boys). The children stand side-by-side and tie the two middle legs together. The children have to use the legs that are tied together to help each other run. The first pair to reach the finish line wins.

Give them some time to practice prior to the race. This is how they will learn that they need to work out a plan to use the middle legs together.

Memory Verse Application:
When God comes into our lives, we need to listen to Him, learn to work together with Him, and run alongside Him to accomplish all He has planned for us!

What happened when one person on the team ran at a different time than the other person? *(Pause for answers)*

Both people fell! That is a good example to show how hard it is to get anywhere in life when we are pulling away from God as His child. Some of us want to live life with God but not really listen to or obey Him. He wants what is best for us. When He gives us instructions, it is always for our good and for His glory.

Alternative Game: Simon Says

Equipment:

None

How to Play the Game:

Children follow directions that are preceded with the phrase "Simon Says." If they choose to follow directions that are given without this phrase, they are out. Keep playing until one person is left. This person becomes "Simon." Play several rounds allowing a different child to be "Simon" each time.

Memory Verse Application:

How does this game remind us of listening to God? We must listen carefully to God's voice and follow His directions and call on our life.

DAY FOUR

Transformation Station

INFILTRATION SERVICE PROJECT

Do something that will share Jesus with others.

Remember:

The importance of this activity is to teach the children the value of reaching out to others, so no matter the activity you choose, point to the fact that this gift will be given to share the love of Jesus with others. You can write a note for each gift to be delivered and have the children sign it. A note might say something like, "At VBS this week, we learned about the gift God gave us when He sent Jesus to be our Savior and Friend. We wanted to share Jesus' love with you, in hopes that it would make you smile. Remember, God loves you so very much!"

Ideas:

- Make peanut butter and birdseed bird feeders for those in a retirement home to be able to see the beautiful birds. This is one way to say we care and you are not forgotten.
- Prepare dry soup mixes in jars or zip top plastic bags to give to the hungry. The ingredients could be donated prior by church members.
- Prepare dry cookie or cake mixes in jars or zip top plastic bags to give to those in the church's neighborhood, inviting them to come to church Sunday. It could be an outreach activity or part of the VBS activity for the older kids or the teens to deliver these (with the approval of parents and supervision of plenty of adults) to the neighborhood on the last day.

DAY FOUR

Closing Skit

Play theme song and memory verse song as children return.

Ask volunteers to share the passcode, memory verse, favorite activity, or something they learned. Or have trivia questions prepared to ask early arrivers.

Begin with the top secret hand signal.

Props & Characters

- 3 chairs
- 1 flashlight
- **1 pair of sunglasses** identical to Tre's, to be presented to Buddy
- **Special Agent Tre** (Code Name: Trinity); dressed like a spy, with a hat and sunglasses
- **Special Agent Buddy** (Code Name: Barnabas); dressed identical to Tre
- **Scout**

Dialogue:

Director: What a great day we had learning that Jesus' call transforms our mission! Let's welcome back our worship leader to review our songs for this week.

(Worship leader sings theme song and today's memory verse song with hand motions.)

Who would like to share one of our passcodes from this week? *(Ask children to share until each day's verse and passcode has been recited.)*

It is a big day for Tre and Buddy. Let's see what they are up to today…

Agent Tre: *(Standing up and announcing in an official voice)* Ladies and gentlemen, today, we have the special privilege of commissioning a brand new agent! Agent Barnabas, please rise.

(Before Buddy stands up, Scout walks in quietly and humbly.)

    Scout: Am I too late?

Agent Tre: *(Huge smile)* No! Not at all! In fact, you are right on time! We were just getting ready to commission our newest agent. Please join us!

Scout: *(Takes a seat on stage)*

Agent Tre: *(Still smiling, repeats in the same tone)* Today, we have the special privilege of welcoming a brand new agent into the family! Agent Barnabas, please rise. *(Buddy stands by Agent Tre)*

Buddy, this week you prayed to receive Jesus' gift of salvation. You accepted Jesus as your Lord and Savior and pledged to follow Him all the days of your life. You were baptized and committed to carefully study the Agent Handbook *(Holds up a Bible)* and to do what it tells you to do. You have been praying and listening carefully to Jesus, our wonderful Boss. In addition, I see you sharing what you have learned with others. It is clear to me and to everyone who knows you that Jesus' love has transformed your identity, Jesus' power has transformed your life, Jesus' presence transforms your choices, and Jesus' call has transformed your mission. We celebrate what God has done in you and what He will now do for others through you.

This flashlight is now yours. May it serve as a constant reminder that Jesus is the light of the world and that the world is filled with people walking in darkness. It is now your lifelong mission to live in the light, to walk in the light, and to share this light with others. If you ever have trouble finding your way, humble yourself, admit where you are, and never be too proud to ask for help. Do you accept this challenge? If so, say, "I do."

Agent Buddy: I do.

Agent Tre: *(Gives Buddy a pair of sunglasses and both put their glasses on)* Everyone, please welcome Special Agent Buddy!

Agent Buddy: *(Nods and mouths "thank you" to everyone)*

Agent Tre: Are you ready?

Agent Buddy: I sure am!

Agent Tre: Then let's go! We've got work to do! *(Both start to head out the door)*

Agent Buddy: *(Stops and turns to Scout)* Hey, friend! Wanna' come along?

Scout: Me? Really? YES! *(Jumps up and steps between them; Tre and Buddy put an arm around Scout's shoulders and all three walk out together)*

Director: God has given us a great last day at *Operation Transformation!* Each day we have celebrated God's transforming love and power! While you were in your Transformation Stations, we counted the offering. Do you want to know who gave the most today, the girls or the boys?

The girls gave $_____ and the boys gave $_____! Way to go! *(Give a report on the total offering for the week and what the children have accomplished. If you had a goal or a special incentive to help kids reach their goal, share it now.)*

(Ask all the volunteers to stand and give children a chance to thank all the workers at VBS with applause. If you are planning a special program, share the details. If possible, plan some extra time during the closing to practice the songs and the passcodes to share in the program. Be sure to have an invitation for children to take home to their families inviting them back to be a part of the program. If a dinner is also happening, be sure the details are provided so that new families understand they are invited.)

Thank You, God, for Your transforming love for each one of us. Thank You for the chance to learn more about You and the chance to help other children around the world. We pray that you will help other children know Your love and Your Son, Jesus! Bring us back together on Sunday to celebrate all You have done this week with our families! In Your Son's name we pray. Amen.

(Remind everyone to invite someone to the program or dinner on Sunday.)

Closing:

Give any other announcements or direction for dismissal. Play theme song as children leave.

MEMORY VERSE ACTIVITIES

OPERATION TRANSFORMATION

Memory Verse Lyrics

THEME SONG

ROMANS 12:2

Do not conform

To the pattern of this world,

But be transformed

By the renewing of your mind.

Then you will be able to attest and approve

What God's will is

His good

Pleasing and perfect will.

Romans 12:2

OPERATION TRANSFORMATION

Memory Verse Hand Motions

THEME SONG

Romans 12:2
* Act like a Roman soldier holding up a spear. Flick two fingers with palm facing inward for the 12. Drop hand with 2 fingers down slowly.

Do not conform to the pattern of this world,
* Act like a robot.

but be transformed
* Bend down a little. Hold hands into chest with clenched fists, then stand up, arms extended high and wide open to show transformation.

by the renewing of your mind.
* Tap forehead with fingers.

Then you
* Point outward to "you."

will be able to test and approve
* Left hand flat. Right hand draws a check mark on left hand.

what God's will is—
* Palms up, fingers curled (to show "want"). Starting up high, slowly lower this hand position showing it is God's will that we are receiving with a renewed mind.

his good,
* Right hand flat, fingers touching chin, then hand moves from chin to other hand. This is the sign language sign for "good."

pleasing
* One hand on tummy, the other hand over the heart, make both hands go around like a bear rubbing it's tummy after eating honey—this is the sign for "pleasing."

and perfect will.
* Palms up, fingers curled (to show "want"). Starting up high, slowly lower this hand position showing it is God's will that we are receiving with a renewed mind.

DAY 1

Opening:
* Snap fingers, nod head, sway.

receive him,
* Clasp hands over heart to show receiving of Him.

who believed in his name,
* Pointer finger right hand taps forehead/temple, then clasp hands. This is the sign language sign for "believe."

children of God.
* Palms down, bouncing on invisible children's heads, then raise hands up to God.

Whistling part:
* Children can whistle, snap, act like they're walking on a sunshiny day, dance in a circle, whatever shows the peace and happiness that comes when we receive Him and become children of God.

Yet to all who did
* Palms up, hands together go down a little, up, then out and down a little showing "all."

to those
* Pointer fingers point out to "those."

he gave the right to become
* Open hands swoop down and draw upward over tummy, stopping over your heart to show the receiving of Him.

John 1:12
* First finger shows 1. For 12, turn palm to self, flick the first and second fingers a couple times (this is sign language for 12).

DAY 2

Opening:
* Snap, sway, smile, then sing!

My sheep
* Palms down, bounce both hands a couple of times to show tapping on the heads of children (God's sheep are people).

listen to my voice;
* Cup hand over one ear on the word "listen," then cup the other hand over the other ear on the word "voice" to show listening.

I know them
* Both hands point to the temple of the forehead to show knowing.

and they follow me.
* Left thumb out in front and higher. Right thumb circles and moves up toward the left thumb "following" the first one.

I give them
* Hands clasped, elbows bent. First swoop right arm from center of your body outward and upward to stop at your head level.

eternal life
* Same as above, but with left hand…swoop left arm from center of your body outward and upward to stop. It is a picture of Jesus on the cross and represents the truth that Jesus' Gift was costly and precious.

and they shall never perish.
* Turn in a circle, rejoicing in this everlasting life Jesus provided us!

John 10:27-28a
* Show 10 fingers, then 7, then 8.

DAY 3

Opening:

* Bob head.

Psalm 25:9

* Open hands like jazz hands to the beat of "Twenty-Five, Nine."

He guides

* Two hands point up at "He," then out at "guides."

the humble

* Left hand on top, laying flat with palm down. Slide right hand underneath (flat hand, palm down), showing humility requires submitting to God, coming under His authority and protection.

in what is right

* Point first fingers on both hands, bounce right hand (at the fist) on top of left hand (at the fist). This is the sign for "right."

and teaches them

* Both hands in the "puppet" position. Fingers flat, bent at the knuckle, thumbs touching first two fingers. We are going to use these hands to show a transfer of information from one person to another. We use this hand position, starting at the forehead (both hands) and move hands out, back in again to the forehead, and out again. Think of a teacher taking information from her head and putting it into the heads of the children.

his way.

* Flat hands, palms facing each other, work together to show a curvy pathway.

Ending:

* Like when a toy's battery goes dead, act like you just ran out of power. Slowly hang head and flop arms.

DAY 4

John 17:3a
* Arms folded for John, bounce head. Right hand, palm forward, touch thumb to ring finger and bounce (this is the sign for 17), then show 3 fingers. (In sign language you use the first two fingers and the thumb to show 3.)

Now this is
* At "this" point right hand to floor. At "is" point left hand to floor.

eternal life:
* One finger pointing up goes around twice (like "This Little Light of Mine"). This means forever. With the same hand, pull your first finger in, put your thumb and pinky finger out making a "y," turn your palm to face forward, and slide your whole hand out, away from the person. This means continuous and never ending. Keep this hand up and point for next part!

that they know you,
* Point first finger on right hand up, pointing at the sky by the time you sing "you."

the only true God,
* Point first finger on left hand and point out and then up, pointing at the sky by the time you sing "true."

* Both hands come down when you say "God."

and Jesus Christ...
* Palms open, taking your pointer or middle finger on one hand, touch the middle of the other hand's palm. This reminds us of the nails in Jesus' hand. Then do the same with the other hand. So that on "Jesus" you touch one palm and on "Christ" you touch the other palm.

Spoken section:
* Bend down, with first finger point to your hand 4 times to the music.
Point to your temple 4 times.
Point to the sky 4 times.
Then stand with arms crossed for reference and do 17:3 like before.

BONUS SONG

1 Timothy 6:18
* Start with a hula hand motion, left and then right. On "18" both hands, palms raise in the air, pumping upward.

Command them
* Right hand, pointer finger points to mouth/chin, then points forward and "lands" on left hand. This is "command" in sign language.

to do good,
* Both thumbs up.

to be rich in good deeds
* Bend at the knees. With your hands palms down, make them go back and forth. (This is the sign language sign for "do" or "doing".)

and to be generous
* Both hands start closed at the heart and open as they alternate right hand, then left hand outward showing "giving" in generosity.

and willing to share.
* Both palms up, see saw forward and back toward the body and away from the body, showing "sharing".

BONUS SONG

Psalm 46:1

* On "1," palms together at your chest, elbows out. Hands are making a "1."

God is our

* Point up for "God," then thumbs point to self for "our."

refuge and strength,

* Step back, cross hands over heart for "refuge," then punch forward for "strength."

[echo] refuge and strength

* Fists clasped yell "refuge and strength" while punching the air above your head.

an ever-present help

* Open hands make a big circle up around and down showing "ever-present."

in trouble.

* Flat hands almost karate style in front of face. With palms down and thumbs in tight to the hand, the right hand comes from in front of forehead and moves down in front of chin on "trou-." Then left does the same thing. Moves down from in front of forehead to in front of chin on "-ble." This is actually the sign language word for "trouble."

OPERATION TRANSFORMATION

Memory Verse Games

MISSING WORDS

You will need a chalkboard, white board, or paper for this activity.

Write the memory verse on a chalkboard or marker board. Ask the children to recite the verse. Choose a volunteer to go and to erase one word. Lead the children as they recite the verse again (including the missing word). Continue this until all the words disappear. If a chalkboard or marker board is not available, write each word of the verse on a separate piece of paper, and ask the children to remove one word at a time.

BIBLE PASS

You will need a Bible and a source of music for this activity.

Have the children sit in a circle. Give one child the Bible. When the music starts, tell the children to pass the Bible around the circle. When the music stops, the child holding the Bible says the Bible verse. Strategically stop the music so each child has an opportunity to say the verse.

BIBLE VERSE RACE

Before the lesson, write each word or phrase of the Bible verse and the reference on a piece of paper. Make two sets.

Divide the class into two teams. Scramble the cards so that the words are out of order. Place a set of word cards on the floor in front of each team. At your signal, the first child on each team will find the first word of the verse and run to a goal line. He or she places the card on the floor and races back to the second player. The second child finds the second word of the verse and races with it to the goal line, placing it in order next to the first word. Continue until one team completes the verse in perfect order. Allow time for the second team to complete its verse. Then have both teams recite the verse together.

BIBLE VERSE LINE

Before the lesson, write each word or phrase of a Bible verse on a separate piece of paper.

Distribute the words to different children, and scatter them throughout the room. Choose one child to arrange the words in order by tagging each individual child holding the words. Then have the class read the verse together.

HIDE AND SEEK

Before the lesson, write each word or phrase of a Bible verse on a separate piece of paper. Then, hide the pieces of paper around the room before the children arrive.

Have the children search the room for the pieces of paper and bring them back to the front. Arrange the words in order, and then ask the class to recite the verse together.

CHAMPION & CHALLENGER

Choose two children who think that they know the memory verse. Stand them back to back in front of the group. One child will start by saying the first word of the verse. Then, the other child will say the second word. Continue back and forth until one child makes a mistake. The other child is the "champion." Ask the whole class to say the memory verse. Then, select a new "challenger," and repeat the game. Soon, both children will be able to complete the memory verse without error.

MEMORY VERSE TOSS

You will need a small ball for this activity.

Ask the children to stand and arrange them in a large circle. Tell the children that whoever catches the ball has to say the next word in the memory verse. Toss the ball to one child to start. He or she recites the first word and then tosses the ball to another child until the entire verse is recited properly. Repeat the game and encourage the children to complete the verse faster each time.

THE REPEATER

Write one or two words of the verse on a small piece of paper.

Instruct students to sit in a circle, and distribute the papers around the circle in correct verse order. Prepare more than one set of memory cards for large classes, and work in groups. The student with the first word of the verse says the first word. Then the next student says the first word and the new word. The third student says the first, second and third words, and so on. Keep repeating the verse from the beginning, adding a new word each time. After you complete the verse, have students pass their card to the person on their left and begin the game again.

BALLOON POP

You will need balloons, a permanent marker, and tape. Blow up the balloons and write one word of the Bible verse on each balloon. Attach the balloons to the wall in correct order.

Let the children read the verse together. Select one child to pop one balloon. Have the children recite the verse again, and remember to say the missing word. Select another child to pop a balloon. Let the children say the verse again. Continue until all the balloons are gone, and the children can recite the verse from memory.

BIBLE VERSE UNSCRAMBLE

Write each word or phrase of a Bible verse on a piece of paper.

Distribute the word cards in mixed order. Let the children arrange themselves in a circle in the correct order according to the portion of the verse they received. Have the children say the verse together. Then ask one child to turn the card around, so the other children cannot see his or her word. Have the children say the verse again. Continue in this manner until all the cards are turned around and no words are visible. This could also be played as a race between two or more teams to see which one is the first to arrange themselves with the words of the verse in the correct.

COLORING PAGES

NOW THIS IS **ETERNAL LIFE:** THAT THEY KNOW YOU, THE ONLY TRUE GOD AND JESUS CHRIST...

John 17:3a

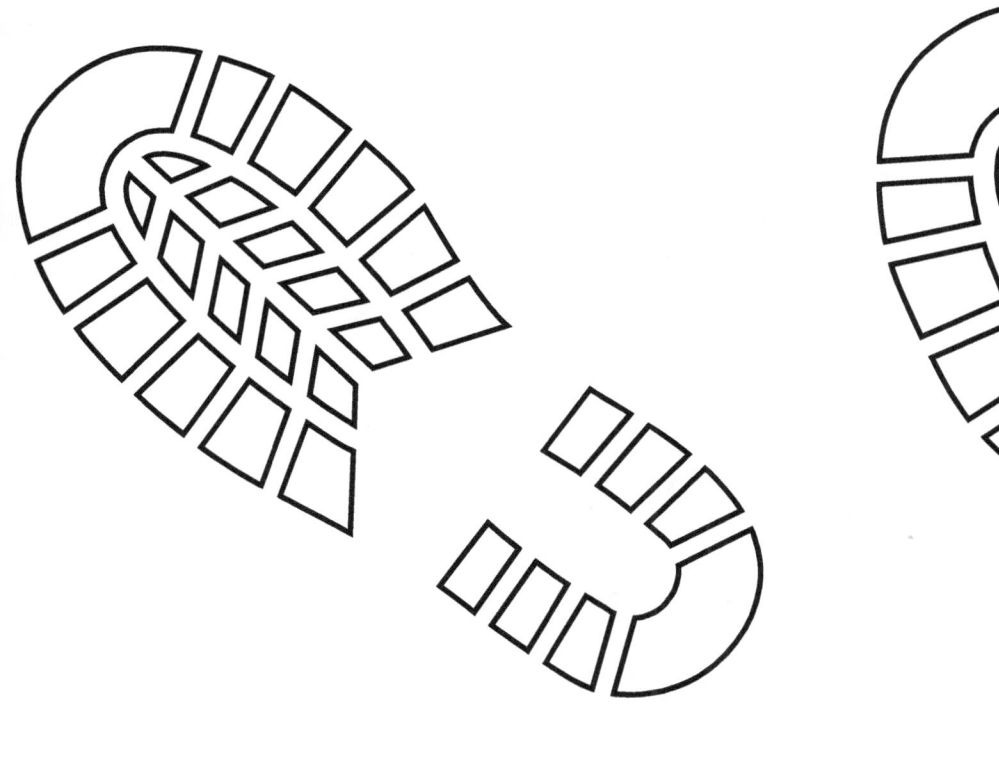

MY SHEEP
LISTEN TO
MY VOICE;
I KNOW THEM,
AND THEY
FOLLOW ME.

John 10:27

Yet to all who did receive him, to those who believed in his name, he gave the right to become children of God.

JOHN 1:12

GRAPHICS, MISC.

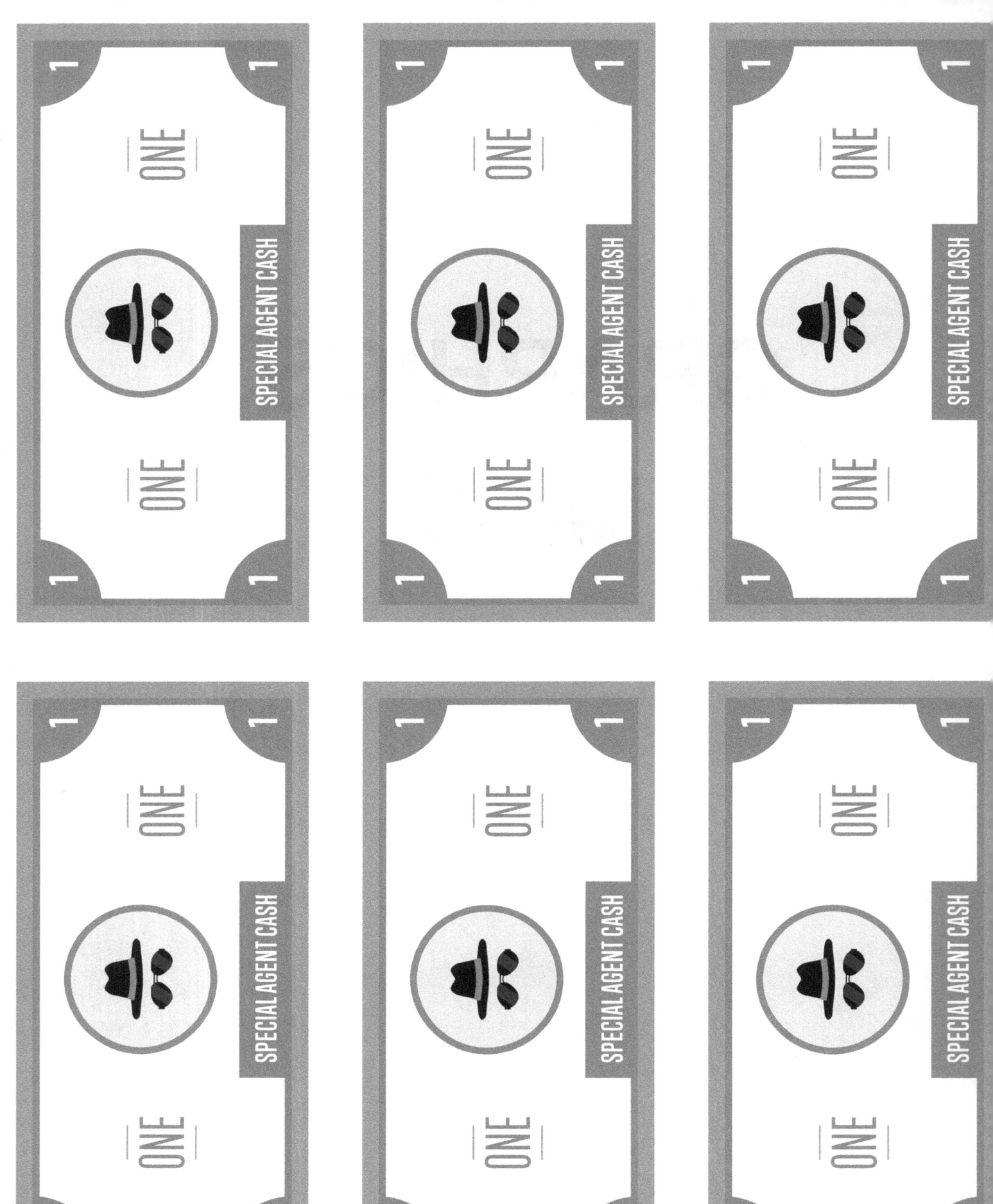

TOP SECRET

TOP SECRET

TOP SECRET

TOP SECRET

SPECIAL AGENT
MISSION
HEADQUARTERS

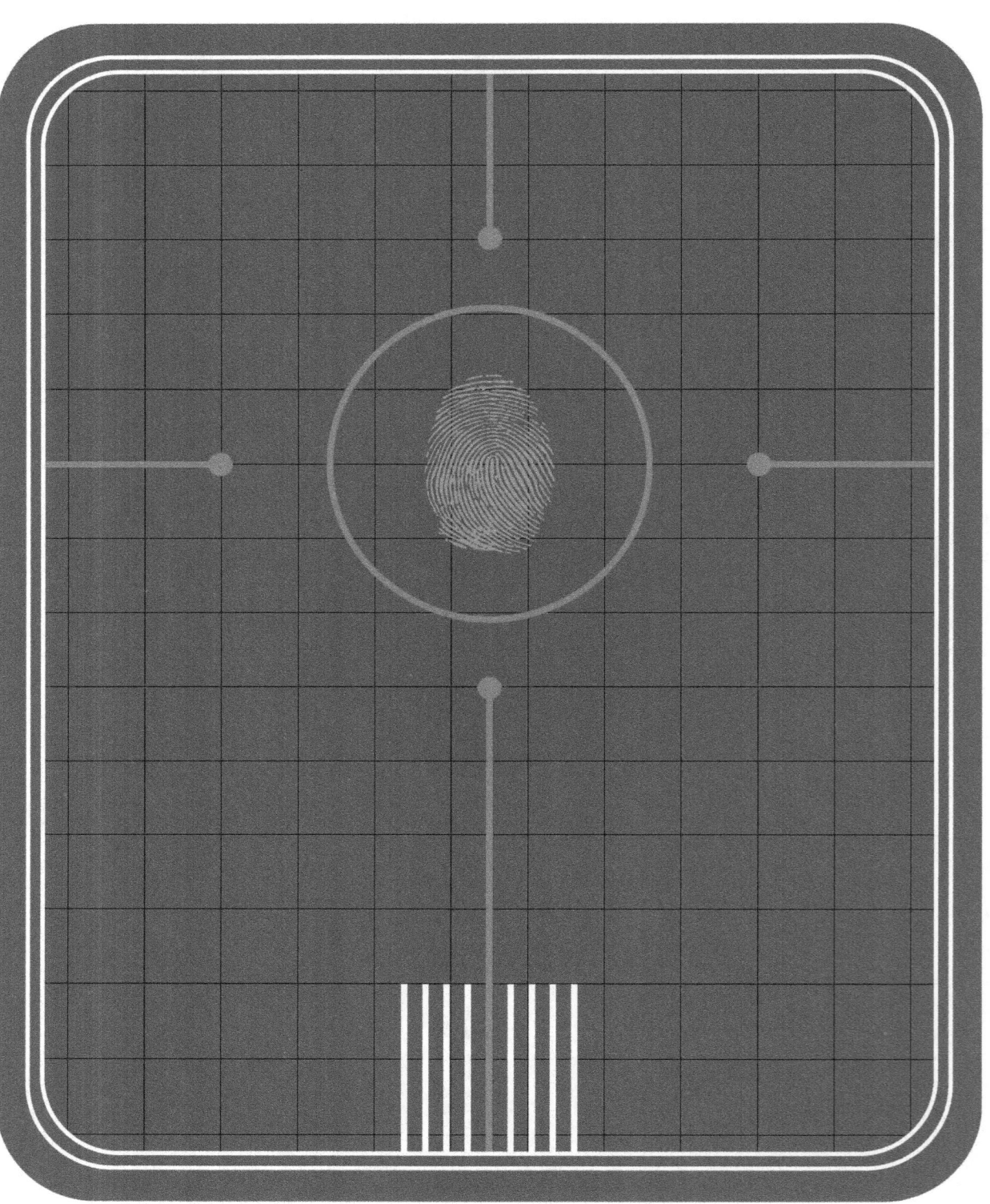

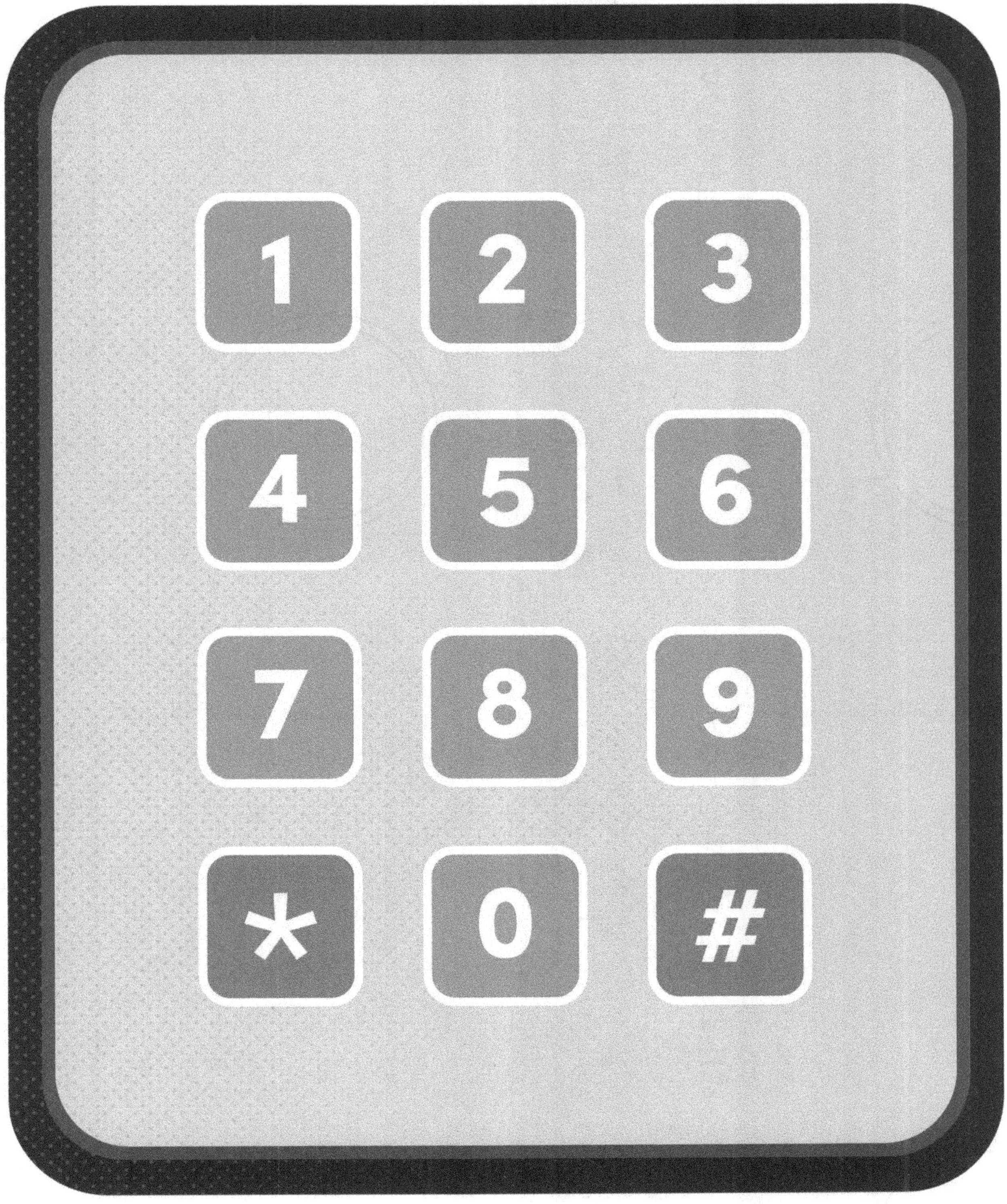
1 2 3
4 5 6
7 8 9
* 0 #

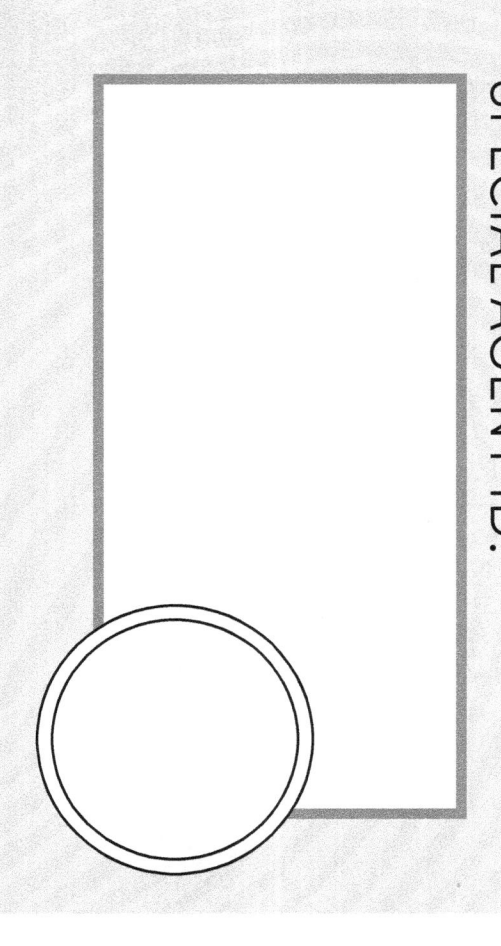
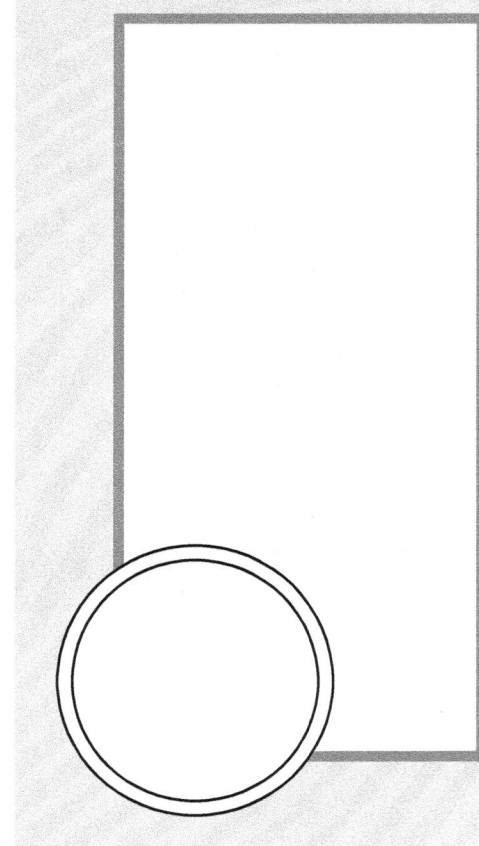
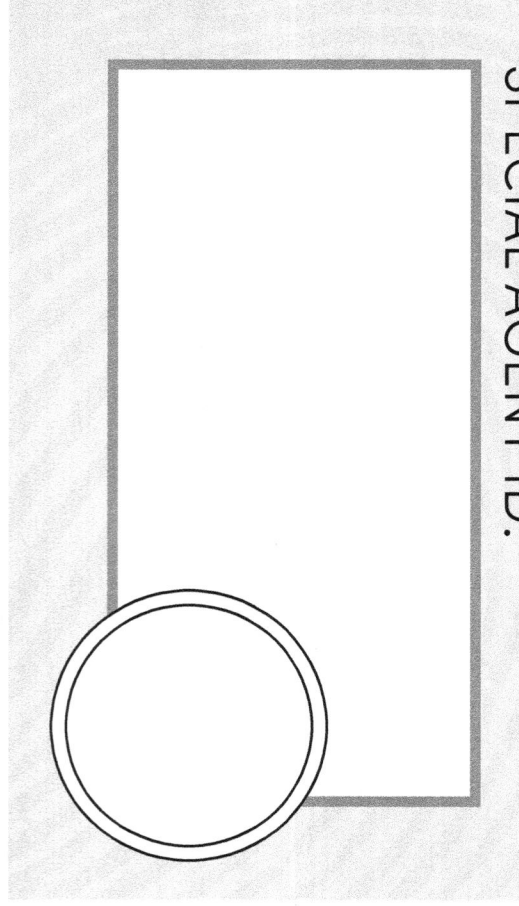

PHONE NUMBER:

PARENT/GUARDIAN:

PHONE NUMBER:

PARENT/GUARDIAN:

PHONE NUMBER:

PARENT/GUARDIAN:

PHONE NUMBER:

PARENT/GUARDIAN:

Memory Verse Chart

NAMES

THEME: Romans 12:2
Do not conform to the pattern of this world, but be transformed by the renewing of your mind. Then you will be able to test and approve what God's will is, his good, pleasing and perfect will.

DAY 1: John 1:12
Yet to all who did receive him, to those who believed in his name, he gave the right to become children of God.

DAY 2: John 10:27-28a
My sheep listen to my voice; I know them and they follow me. I give them eternal life and they shall never perish.

DAY 3: Psalm 25:9
He guides the humble in what is right and teaches them his way.

DAY 4: John 17:3
Now this is eternal life: that they know you, the only true God, and Jesus Christ, whom you have sent.

BONUS: 1 Timothy 6:18
Command them to do good, to be rich in good deeds and to be generous and willing to share.

BONUS: Psalm 46:1
God is our refuge and strength, an ever-present help in trouble.

OPERATION TRANSFORMATION

www.ingramcontent.com/pod-product-compliance
Lightning Source LLC
Chambersburg PA
CBHW081346040426
42450CB00015B/3317